2·50

14

THE AGE OF THE TRACTION ENGINE

ROBERT A. WHITEHEAD

First published 1970

ISBN 1-85648-189-1

First published 1970 by Ian Allan Ltd
This edition published 1994
By Fraser Stewart Book Wholesale Ltd,
Waltham Abbey, Essex.
Produced by the Promotional Reprint Company Limited.

Printed in India

Contents

Preface

THE PREFACE is the part of the book which the reader, if he reads it at all, reads first and which the author writes last. Thus the latter has full knowledge of the sins he has committed in the pages that follow and is able to allay, he hopes, the reader's critical instincts by preparing him for what is to come.

This is not intended to be a work of erudition and is not based upon profound research though it is founded upon a reasonable knowledge of the subject. Its purpose is to amuse rather than to instruct and if the anecdotes related in the following pages bring a smile to the face of the non-technical reader and a chuckle to the old engineman, I shall feel my labour has not been in vain.

To record the bare facts of history is one thing but to try to record the spirit or feeling that brought about those facts or which the facts in their turn prompted is a different matter. It is this that I have attempted and the result is offered to the reader with the utmost diffidence in the knowledge that at best all I can have done is to give a glimpse or a hint of what that great and complicated tapestry, the nineteenth century, was like.

War Department engines have been deliberately and rigidly excluded from this book. This is a subject of immense interest and intricacy and there is an abler pen than mine about to be put to work on a book devoted to this subject.

Friends are a great help in writing a book. To these I am very greatly indebted—first, to Tom Paisley, who has allowed his immense collection of photographs to be ransacked for this book and who has also, with great patience, talked over the subject matter and read the draft; and second (but only for alphabetical reasons) to the Reverend Reuel C. Stebbing, who was an engineer before he was a parson, and who gave much help in the initial stages as well as reading the completed manuscript.

Particular thanks are due to friends in the Road Locomotive Society—Messrs R. G. Pratt (past chairman), A. Duke (Engine Records Officer), E. E. Kimbell, A. J. Martin (both committee members), W. S. Love (Honorary Secretary), J. C. Butler, C. Hooker, W. W. Martin, W. Roberts and J. P. Mullett.

As in my other ventures into print my wife, Jean, has done a great deal of the actual work of putting the book together and our friend Beryl Beale has typed the manuscript—help which has been immensely valuable.

My thanks are due to those who have provided the illustrations. Generally these are individually acknowledged—where no acknowledgement appears the photograph is either from Tom Paisley's collection or my own.

Finally to all who have helped in any degree, whether mentioned or not, I send my heartiest thanks.

ROBERT A. WHITEHEAD

Tonbridge, Kent.
November 1969

An engraving, issued by the makers, of Aveling's first traction engine after his experiments in making the Clayton & Shuttleworth portable self-moving

[J. P. Mullet collection

CHAPTER I

Origins and Makers

"The necessary perfection in boilers, in the mechanism of the steam engine, the convenient disposition of the component parts of the machine . . . are not likely to be attained by any individual".

The Penny Cyclopaedia.
VOL. XXII, 1838

CUGNOT constructed his celebrated three wheeled steam tractor for the haulage of guns in 1769 and demonstrated it in 1770. Though it was not a true success it worked well enough to complete a demonstration; it still exists. The bi-centenary of steam on roads is thus a matter of months away at the time of writing and it is perhaps salutory to remember that the traction engine as we know it appeared when the first of these two centuries was all but accomplished.

Though the traction engine is an easy thing to recognise it is a difficult machine to define. For the purpose of this book it is taken as the four-wheeled, locomotive boilered, over-type engine with which we are now familiar at rallies and capable, in contrast to the self-moving portable, of hauling an independent payload of at least twice its own weight. As a definition this is clearly full of loopholes but it is a workable guideline.

The bias of the development work put into road steam from the time of Cugnot's experiments, until about 1840 was towards the carriage of passengers. Murdoch, the devoted employee of Watt, who might have turned his talents to the haulage of goods rather than the drainage of mines or the development of gas lighting, was deterred from this course by Watt's disapproval. Nevertheless, he built a model road locomotive at Redruth between 1781 and 1784 that was intended to haul a model wagon, as

was a second and larger one which he constructed in 1792. Both models were three wheeled, with vertical boiler in which the single vertical cylinder was set, the piston driving an oscillating beam from which a second rod drove the cranked axle. He is reputed (1792-1794) to have gone on to build a steam carriage, an application that was carried further by Trevithick, the Cornish engineer, who knew Murdoch and probably appreciated his pioneer work. Trevithick's two carriages of 1801 and 1803 used higher pressure steam than Murdoch's but failed to make any marked impact—commercially or socially.

The first man to make a commercially usable steam road vehicle was almost certainly Walter Hancock of Stratford, Essex, who built a number of vertical boilered rear engined steam carriages which he put into service in the metropolis for five years or so, beginning in 1831. These vehicles were crude by latter day standards just as the railway locomotive of the period was crude but there can be no reasonable doubt that had the steam road carriage been allowed to evolve with the same freedom as the railway locomotive it would have arrived, as quickly, at a thoroughly workable form. However, public opinion and the legislature were not yet ready for the steam carriage and by the successive Turnpike Acts of the 1830's it was legislated out of existence except as a toy.

In 1829, a Mr Isaac Brown of East Morton, Yorkshire, had made a steam "mechanical horse" for coupling to existing horse-drawn vehicles and it is reputed to have been capable of hauling six people. Hancock went further, in 1834, in constructing a steam "drag", a tractor based on his principles, but again this was a comparatively light machine aimed mainly at drawing passenger carriages.

Other builders or inventors of steam carriage in this period included Griffith (1821), Gordon (1822), Gurney, Burstall & Hill, James Summers and Ogle, Heaton, Church, Dance & Field, Squire & Macerone, Scott Russell, Hill, and Anderson. They were on the whole an ingenious and disputatious set of men. With the exception of Gurney, whose carriages worked a service between Gloucester and Cheltenham from February to May, 1831 before being driven off the road by the opposition of the turnpike trusts, and of Russell who ran one for a while from Glasgow to Paisley, none of the others had anything like the success of Hancock and never ran a vehicle in regular public service.

Though these carriages were interesting machines whose suppression was a sad waste of opportunity, their relevance to the traction engine was slight. The first moves in the true direction of the traction engine was the Ransomes' self-propelled threshing machine exhibited at the Royal Show at Bristol in 1842 in which the road wheels could be coupled by a pitch chain to the engine. The engine was on Davies' disc principle, an early attempt to supersede the reciprocating engine, and took its power from a vertical boiler; though it performed moderately well and took a prize of £30 it never found a purchaser. The same firm returned to the struggle in 1849, when the Royal was at Leeds, showing Robert Willis' "Farmers' Engine", a light undertype traction engine with two $6\frac{1}{4}$in $\times$ 10in cylinders placed under the smokebox. The engine, built for Ransomes by E. B. Wilson and Company of the Railway Foundry, Leeds, was a neat design

carefully executed but failed by being too lightly made for the duty it had to perform—threshing. Nevertheless, it was capable of running a distance of twelve miles in one hour and showed what was possible.

After this attempt to design a traction engine from first principles, interest seems to have turned back or to have been more acutely focussed upon the idea of making the common portable engine self-moving.

In fact, the increasing use of the portable engine had posed to many active minds, including that of Thomas Aveling (who has left a record of his thoughts on the subject), the absurdity of a relatively powerful prime mover being dragged with more or less difficulty about the countryside by a team of horses.

Richard Bach of Birmingham, a builder of portable engines, converted one to geared drive in 1855 and fitted it with Boydell patent wheels, the forerunner of the modern tracked vehicle. Richard Garrett and Sons of Leiston did the same a few months later with an engine which was shown at the Royal Show at Chelmsford in 1856. Another builder who offered his portables as self-movers, using the method of chain drive patented by Williams in 1857, was John Smith of Coven, Staffordshire. This village manufacturer of inventive mind never achieved more than a modest success before his death at the relatively early age of 52 in 1879. Clayton & Shuttleworth built two chain driven ploughers for Fowler in 1858.

The idea of the chain drive added to an otherwise ordinary portable engine now began to be applied by several manufacturers—Garretts in 1858, Thomas Aveling in 1859, followed by Savage, Dodman, Burrell, Tuxford, Clayton & Shuttleworth, Tasker, Lampitt and others, gradually evolving into a distinct species, which (except for Tuxford who used a vertical enclosed engine) retained in the main the characteristic portable engine arrangement of cylinders over the firebox with crankshaft carrying a large flywheel just behind the chimney, but in other respects gradually

A well-known photograph of an Aveling chain drive
traction engine of the early eighteen-sixties showing
the fifth wheel-steering and the abominable arrangement of the chain sprocket stuck out from the firebox
on a stub shaft from a single bracket, the same shaft
carrying the drive pinion

A very early picture, probably dating from the
'seventies, of a Savage "Agriculturist" traction
engine. The rear wheels contained a central trough
cast into the periphery. When the rear of the engine
was jacked up the wheels could be used as the winding
drums of a "roundabout" ploughing outfit. When not
thus used, the trough was covered

[R. G. Pratt collection

Front steered chain engine by Charles Burrell, in general conception very similar to the Savage but in detail quite
different. The wheels are of wrought iron of built-up construction where those of the Savage are cast, the flywheel
is the opposite hand and the manstand and tanks differ

[Dr. J. Middlemiss collection

acquiring the outline of the authentic traction engine. Thus the rudimentary footplate and separate tender of the early Savage chain-engines developed into a manstand with tank and bunkers of the true traction engine form. Steering, too, progressed from the straight-forward horse-steering via the Aveling fifth-wheel arrangement and front steerage by ship's wheel and chains to the long-lived chain and bobbin steering worked from the manstand. Methods of final drive varied, the concensus being with a countershaft driving via an annular gear on the inner periphery of the rear wheel.

In this respect the Ransomes' "Farmers' Engine" gave a lead that several others were to follow. John Smith of Coven, who produced chain-engines with cylinders above the firebox, also produced an under type engine in which the locomotive type boiler was pivoted about its centre of gravity on a carrying frame to which the cylinder block was attached and in which the final drive was by chain from a sprocket on the crankshaft to a larger sprocket bolted to the rear wheel. William Bray of Folkestone, founder of Brays Traction Engine Company was responsible for a number of

An engraving from the catalogue of the Russell company in the USA twenty years later than the picture of Aveling's first traction engine but still using basically the same layout, though horse steerage has taken the place of the fifth wheel. The engine has a separate tender and is hauling a Massillon thresher

[J. P. Mullett collection

In the 1863 Smithfield Show, Fowler showed a 10hp plougher with steerage from the manstand. It was severely criticised by the "*Engineer*". This same engine also had a gear drive to which the "*Engineer*" also took exception saying drive should be by chain and steerage at the front.

The chain used in these engines was the crude and unreliable pitch chain of the period. Had the modern roller chain been available it is quite probable that the course of traction engine design might have been different but as it was the shortcomings of the chains of the period deflected attention to the all gear drives.

engines with all-gear drive, some under-mounted, from 1856 into the early 1860s in conjunction with D. K. Clark who was consulting engineer to his company. Clark went on designing isolated examples of the undertype engine until about 1877. Like most undertypes, his engines had a high weight to power ratio but otherwise were well designed and put together for their period. Again his latter engines were the product of railway engine builders, Dübs & Company of Glasgow.

During the early 'sixties, undertype engines were built by Hornsby and Sons, using final drive by chain, Fisken Brothers of Leeds, John

Early front steered chain drive Savage for Samuel Wright, Barrowden, Rutland, photographed at Kings Lynn [Ronald H. Clark collection

The successor to the chain engine. Still front steered, this double cylindered Clayton & Shuttleworth, No 9338, 1869, owned by Henry Smith, Cropwell Grove, was 10nhp and had all gear drive with three shafts

[F. Gilford

An extremely rare photograph of Bray's original traction engine of 1857, photographed in 1859. Bray, the designer, is the man in the stove-pipe hat near the front wheel

[J. P. Mullett collection

Fowler & Company and finally by Marshalls of Gainsborough. Fiskens' engine, to the designs of a Mr. Willsher, avoided a separate chassis and worked reasonably well—well enough, in fact, for an example to survive at work until as late as 1914—but had a complicated arrangement of countershaft within a hollow rear axle and the flywheel concentric with the nearside rear wheel but just clear of it on the outside. Marshall's undertype of 1876, the company's first essay in traction engine building, suffered from the additional dead-weight of a steel chassis and a high centre of gravity of the boiler. Other builders of the period who produced undertype engines were Taylor of Birkenhead, Dunston Engine Works, Gateshead (Archer and Hall's patent), and Chaplin of Glasgow, who used a vertical boiler. The list is not exhaustive and merely illustrates that many well-qualified contenders tackled the problem of the undermounted engine. Because of its weight this type of engine was not well suited to agricultural work. A number of examples, moreover, having no accessible flywheel, were intended solely for road haulage, a field of endeavour virtually closed to steam by the 1865 Locomotive Act. Examples of the undermounted engine appeared at intervals, and as late as the Royal Show at Norwich in 1886, Fowler exhibited a Whittingham patent under-

The Whittingham patent four-wheeled drive traction engine built by Fowler in 1886

[John Fowler & Co

type traction engine on four equal sized wheels, all driven. Again the engine was solely for haulage and proved unsaleable.

The parallel development of the chain-engine had led to something more hopeful, however. Early in the eighteen sixties a number of makers had transposed the cylinder block and crankshaft from the conventional portable engine position so that the crankshaft was over the firebox and a much shorter chain was thus needed. In 1861, Aveling attempted to patent the arrangement of the cylinder within the dome at the smokebox end. Possibly Clayton & Shuttleworth was the first firm to do this but others quickly followed—notably Aveling & Porter, Richard Garrett & Sons, Brown & May of Devizes and Tasker of Andover. The arrangement had been used for at least five years previously, however, in the Boydell engines built by Charles Burrell at Thetford which had, in addition, an all-gear drive. Burrell's engines were more successful than Boydell's wheels which hammered themselves to pieces whenever used at more than a crawl, a good case of the inventor's vision having outrun his, and his contemporaries', technology. In the nature of the ground it could traverse and the load it could haul, the Boydell engine was first class, but the whole conception was defeated finally by inability to keep the wheels economically in repair.

Yet another parallel line of evolution was taking place in steam ploughing engines. Ploughing by steam is outside the scope of this book and it is sufficient to say that the man whose inventiveness and initiative did more than any other to make it a success was John Fowler. At the outset Fowler had not intended to be a manufacturer and contented himself with having his plant built by established manufacturers, one of which firms was Kitson, Thompson & Hewitson, the railway engine builders of Leeds (others were Ransomes, Clayton & Shuttleworth and Robert Stephenson). When Fowler commenced building engines at his own factory in Leeds established in 1860, his own high quality of inventiveness and his happy choice of associates were reinforced by the standards that had been set in the Kitson engines. From 1864 onwards John Fowler offered for sale his single-cylindered ploughing engine with cylinder behind the chimney, crankshaft carried in cast iron brackets over the firebox and all-gear drive to the rear axle.

David Greig, Fowler's partner and designer of the steam engines built by the firm, patented in 1868 an arrangement of the crank and counter shafts in a cast iron combined frame bolted to the outside crownplate of the firebox, though it is doubtful it if was applied to an actual engine.

The Earl and Countess of Caithness with The Rev. William Ross of Kintore on the front seat of the steam carriage built by Thomas Rickett (seen on the rear platform) at the Castle Foundry, Buckingham. The photograph was presumably taken on the occasion of their drive from Inverness to Barrogill Castle near Thurso (approximately 150 miles) on August, 3 to 6, 1860   [A. S. Heal collection

Almost all the ingredients of the modern traction engine had thus been assembled in one machine. The final constituent was supplied by Thomas Aveling in his design of 1870—the upward extension of the firebox side plates to form a crank-box with a cast iron frame inside to receive the crankshaft and countershaft bearing brackets. Aveling patented this idea but in fact it had been anticipated in the form in which it was subsequently used i.e. without the inner cast iron frame as was established by J. and H. McLaren in the defence in the historic case brought against them by Aveling in February 1881 alleging infringement. Though most of the constituent parts of the Aveling innovation had been used before by others he was, in fact, the first manufacturer to place an engine on the market in the enduring form.

The Aveling engine of 1870 brought together what the author submits are the essential ingredients of the typical traction engine: steam-jacketed cylinders at the leading end of the locomotive-type boiler which formed the chassis, crank- and countershaft in a crank-box integral with the firebox side plates, all-gear drive and steering by chain and bobbin from the man-stand, under which was placed the water tank and upon which the coal was carried in a bunker behind the driver. This design left

behind the steering by horse in shafts, the "fifth wheel" or pilot steerage, the steerage by ships wheel, bevels and chains by a steersman placed on a platform before the smokebox, steerage by rack and pinion or, as in certain ploughing engines direct chain steerage—"tank steerage" and all the other devices that had been employed. Though it is by no means certain who first used it, certainly most makers recognised the Aveling design as a good idea and adopted it within a few years. Thus it must be recognised that although it had some defects—notably placing the steersman far back, making his task extremely tiring, because of the slack in the chain at higher speeds—it had the qualities that appealed to the threshing contractor. These attractions were low initial cost, freedom from damage on rough ground because the chains could be left fairly slack, ease of adjustment and the placing of driving and steering together—an important point in awkward manoeuvres, such as setting to the drum, where the driver may wish to steer as well.

Three refinements remained to be accomplished—the use of the differential gear, compounding and road springs. The differential seems to have been used in the steam carriage built by Roberts in 1825 but was adopted only slowly in traction engines, probably because of the additional weight, complication and the expense. It did not become general in fact, until the end of the 'nineties, mainly because, until the advent of the alleviating clause of the Locomotive Act of 1896, it was practically impossible to use a traction engine for anything outside agriculture or parochial haulage where the removal of the driving pin from one wheel at really sharp turns was not a crippling disadvantage. On a soft-surfaced road a little wheel slip to compensate for the absence of a differential took place easily, though it was less easily tolerated on properly surfaced town roads.

Compounding in portables was inaugurated by Richard Garrett & Sons in 1879, the first compound portable appearing at the Royal Show at Derby in that year. The use of compounding in traction engines was introduced by Fowler in 1881 but was effectually brought into use by the remarkable performance put up by Edwin Foden's compound traction engine at the trials organised by the Royal Agricultural Society at Newcastle in 1887. At the same trials, Thomas Cooper of Ryburgh entered a chain-driven engine built for him at Leiston Works by Garrett, the last of the old type chain engines to be shown in public. As a matter of interest, the chain-driven haulage engine never

became entirely defunct, continuing a tenuous existence marked by a few isolated examples such as the Mason & Weyman vertical-boilered tractor. In the early years of the new century, chain-driven tractors by Foden, Nayler and Tasker appeared using roller chain, after the invention of which chain-drive received a new popularity.

Springs were a different matter. Front axles could readily be fitted with a single transverse spring in a slotted carriage jaw. The springing of main driving axles was more difficult because of the movement introduced into the gear train. Some firms, of whom Garretts and Wallis & Steevens are examples, limited spring travel to about ⅜in which could be taken up in the gearing without the teeth coming out of mesh. Other makers, such as Burrell, Foden and Fowler devised systems permitting much greater movement but at the expense of greater cost and complication that made such springing a poor economic proposition in an engine intended to spend most of its life statically driving a threshing machine with short journeys between bouts over softish roads. As with compounding, the springing of engines acquired

*These engines have been very fully described and illustrated by T. B. Paisley in his history of the firm—"The Fowells of St Ives".

The first compound traction engine built in the United Kingdom: Fowler No 4162 of 1881

[John Fowler & Co

A minor make that was extremely durable. Fowell 7nhp No 93 (CE 7894) of 1904 photographed in circa 1912 with its owner, J. P. Charter of Comberton, Cambs, on the footplate. Fowell set the perch bracket well back to give a small turning circle for the narrow fen lanes—the engines were made at St Ives, Hunts, in the fens commercial significance only after the 1896 Act had made road haulage possible on a serious scale.

The solving of the springing problem produced several interesting variants of the conventional traction engine layout. The most significant commercially was that designed by Thomas Box of Uffington, Berkshire in which power was transmitted by gearing to a jackshaft beneath the belly of the boiler and thence by side connecting rods, not unlike those of a railway engine, to the rear axle. No differential was used but the drive was transmitted through friction bands that could be slackened on one side or the other for sharp bends. Box engines were built mostly by the small firm of Fowell of St Ives, Huntingdonshire*.

Whilst the traction engine was in its formative years from 1870 to 1900, numerous variations were designed and some patented, the longest lived of which was the three-wheeled layout either with a locomotive boiler or, more importantly, with a vertical boiler. Fowler built three-wheeled engines of which the famous *Progress* of the Cheadle Carrying Company in Staffordshire is probably best known but the series of engines most entitled to fame are the road steamers, combining the three-wheel layout with the vertical boiler and resilient rubber tyres invented by their designer

Robert William Thomson, (1822—1873), an Edinburgh engineer. His death from locomotor ataxy at the age of fifty-one removed from the scene an inventor who, had he lived, might have had a profound influence on road engine design. Thomson was not a manufacturer and his engines were built variously by Nairn, Tennant, Burrell, Robey and Ransomes, Sims & Head. Thomson locomotives were given an extended trial on road trains in India under the direction of Lt (later Lt Col) Crompton. By an unhappy coincidence the death of Thomson in 1873 and the departure of Crompton from India in 1875 came at a time when the Government of India was debating the relative merits of steam road trains and the metre-gauge light railway, coming down on the side of the latter. As has been noticed, steam road haulage in Great Britain stagnated between 1865 and 1896 so that as a result of the Indian decision following on the untimely removal of Thomson, the production of his road steamers came to an end and with it virtually the era of the three-wheeled engine. Three-wheeled engines of otherwise conventional layout had little advantage over four-wheelers because of the concentration of weight on the single wheel and the fact that on narrow country lanes it tended to run on and off the horse-path between the wheel ruts into which a four-wheeler fitted

The three-wheeled traction engine. A single cylinder three-wheeler built by Fowler for road haulage, but the exact date is not known

An unusual engine by a rare maker. Thomson road steamer built by T. M. Tennant & Co of Leith and owned by a Mr White of Kellock's Mill, Aberdeen, from 1870 to 1888, was one of the few traction engines built in Scotland

happily. Examples of Thomson's steamers ran until the present century—a tribute to their fundamental soundness.

The Thomson engines were the last serious deviants from what thereafter became the standard British traction engine. In North America, the only other major area of traction engine production, very different circumstances prevailed. Whereas in Great Britain good skilled engineer's labour was cheap, in North America it was not only very expensive but extremely difficult to obtain. An American traction engine was designed, therefore, to need as little skilled labour in its manufacture as possible with the result that such complicated pieces of machining as crankshafts were abandoned in favour of disc cranks and very little superficial finish was given to the constituent parts.

Perhaps more important even than this influence was that of the pioneering spirit. Despite regional differences, English rural society was remarkably homogeneous and had a tradition of durability that even Tolpuddle and the unrest that followed the Napoleonic Wars had not shaken. The equipment of the English countryside had a long life—windmills, watermills, the blacksmith's bellows, the wagon, the tumbril, barns, stables and houses were all longer lived than their human users—and the English farmer was a man of conservative outlook. The farmer and contractor looked, therefore, for an engine that with proper care and replacement of wearing parts would last a lifetime and when he increased his stock tended to buy a second like the first. The American, by contrast, whether a new immigrant or a first generation American, was, by definition, a man who had repudiated the set social order and

Minnis Crawler of 1869 built by Thomas S. Minnis, Meadville, Pennsylvania and used for breaking virgin ground in Iowa. Note the tracks after the style of R. W. Thomson

[R. G. Pratt collection

Avery 20nhp double-cylinder undermounted traction with eight-furrow plough at the Winnipeg Motor Trials, 1910

[E. R. Potter collection, RLS

Two engines by the Cornell Threshing Co of Brampton, Ontario. The man in white overall is Lewis McEwan, later the Saskatchewan Government boiler inspector. The wheels were of wood with cast-iron face segments. Date—1889

[E. R. Potter collection, RLS

A photograph taken near Winnipeg in 1910 of what is believed to be the first 80bhp Case traction engine, built in December 1909. The ploughs are fitted with a steam lifting device.

[E. R. Potter collection, RLS

Compound Reeves 32nhp traction engine with a ten-bottom Cockshutt gang plough breaking up turf, double discing and harrowing in South Alberta, 1917

[E. R. Potter collection, RLS

conservatism of the old European societies and was pushing out, literally or figuratively, into virgin lands. Such a man bought an engine that would serve him until a better one became available, and he did not look askance, as his English counterpart might have done, at the

bizarre or unorthodox shapes that inventive minds conjured up for American traction engines. This readiness to accept innovation undoubtedly encouraged inventiveness among traction engine builders—whether it ultimately benefited the user is a different question to which the author has no answer.

It needs to be remembered that the use of steam road haulage in America was so slight as to be practically negligible and that the work of traction engines fell broadly into the two classes of threshing and ploughing. Some engines did both but many were confined to threshing and had a greater affinity to the self-moving portable in England rather than to the English traction engine. A low weight to power ratio was encouraged by earth roads and dubious bridges. American builders were capable when necessary of producing rugged machines of great power as witness the huge ploughing traction engines of Case and Avery. Indeed an Avery undermounted engine with its enclosed railway type cab designed to plough the northern wheatlands in the cold of the North American autumn seems to have more of the railway than the road in its outline.

What is perhaps surprising is the durability of American engines not consciously designed for long life. American traction engines forty to sixty years old appear in numbers at American rallies. Yet a further surprise is the astonishing variety of type and arrangement the American species demonstrate—overtypes and under-types on locomotive boilers, engines with simple return flue boilers, vertical boilers, vertical engines, four wheelers and three wheelers in weights from seven or eight tons up to well over thirty—a visual testimony to the toleration displayed by the American user to the idiosyncrasies of the makers.

The American threshing machine was as distinct from its English counterpart as were the American traction engines. The preservation of unbroken straw was seldom of importance in America where vast amounts of it had no better fate than to be burned, either in a bonfire or in the firebox of a straw burning engine. The peg drum machine, therefore, predominated in which the revolving drum had projecting pegs set around its circumference which, as it revolved, passed between similar pegs fixed statically in the body of the machine. Such threshers detached the corn from the ear with great effect but the straw was sadly battered.

In an English thresher the drum had beater bars usually, though not invariably, spirally fluted on the outer face and set along its length parallel to the axis. The drum was adjusted so

A photograph taken in South Alberta in c. 1905 of a Canadian threshing gang assembled in front of their John Abel strawburner, a single-cylinder engine of either 18 or 20hp

[E. R. Potter collection, RLS

Rear-end view of an American Case, threshing in 1910. The engine is a strawburner and the heap of straw in the foreground is its fuel.

[E. R. Potter collection, RLS

that as it revolved there was sufficient clearance between it and the stationary concave for the heads of wheat to be rubbed between the two, separating the corn from the remainder of the ear. The straw passed out on to straw shakers to make sure that no corn remained amongst it, cavings passed over a cavings sieve for the same purpose and were blown out by a fan while the wheat fell to the bottom of the machine from which it was elevated by metal cups on a continuous belt to the top of the machine to pass downwards through a smutter and thence through a rotary screen to the appropriate sack spout, firsts, seconds or tail corn, the dust being blown out by air blast in the process.

The seeder was a modified form of thresher designed to thresh out the seeds of seed grasses and the clover huller was the equivalent machine for use with clover. Seed separation was a much lighter and more delicate task than corn threshing needing much greater attention to close jointing in the machine for whereas a day's output in corn might be 75 sacks or more with seeding it would be reckoned in pounds. It is claimed, probably with justice, that the clover huller marketed by Richard Garrett & Sons Ltd of Leiston in 1896 was the first commercially successful English huller. In this the threshing process was in two stages, carried on in separate drums, the first separating the clover heads from the remainder of the plant and the second rubbing out the seeds from the heads.

Straw issuing from the thresher might pass through a straw tier, which formed it up into trusses of roughly 56 pounds weight, tying each truss with bindertwine. Alternatively, it might drop into a high density baler which would deliver it in wire-bound rectangular bales weighing roughly a hundredweight and a half. Tied straw could be lifted to stack height by a straw elevator or might be simply pitched up on to the stack. Alternatively the straw might go neither through a tier nor baler but into a chaff cutter to be cut into chaff for livestock feeding. Straw chaff provided little, if any, nourishment but was useful in giving animals, particularly horses in stables, something to munch on and to induce a satisfying feeling of repletion which the less bulky nutrient foods did not supply.

Fowler three shaft 6nhp of c. 1880, working at a saw bench when owned by William Mulley, Needham Market, Suffolk

[R. G. Pratt collection

From time to time traction engines provided, on a minor scale, power for a much wider range of machines. Garrett's manufactures included, in addition to engines themselves, sawbenches, tile making machines (for land-drainage tiles), cake crushers, hammer mills (for provender), maize shellers and pumps besides living vans and traction wagons and this was by no means an exceptional range of products. Of all of them the traction wagon was of the widest utility and longest survival, production continuing from the eighteen sixties until World War I and the vehicles themselves remaining in use virtually to the present time. John Fowler & Company, typical of the high class engine builder, offered wagons in five sizes, carrying respectively four, five, six, eight and ten tons, on steel wheels. Some other makers preferred the wooden wheel with steel tyres and iron bushes in the hubs. These latter could be a curse for when the

weather was hot and dry they would work loose in the hub and if the load was heavy they might overheat, leading to the wheel catching fire. All the main framing was of ash and the fore-carriage was built of ash with softwood floor, sides and ends put together with iron tongues. A screw brake with wooden brake blocks mounted on a cross beam was provided on the rear wheels.

The same firm offered also a double side-tipping wagon, a very heavily built "special" wagon for carrying ingots, machine beds or similar items of concentrated weight up to 20 tons, a pole wagon for timber haulage, and an all-steel tender wagon with coal space on top of a large water tank on four heavy iron wheels. Unlike some makers, Fowler would provide springs to order.

Traction wagons were a great standby and were used for purposes as diverse as the most

Burrell 8nhp crane engine in a posed picture outside the works at Thetford. The draped tarpaulin over the building in the background was supposedly thought to be neater than the elevation it covered—one wonders how bad that could have been

The conveyance that took Charles Hooker and his wife from the church where they were married at Egerton at Easter, 1906. The engine was an Aveling & Porter dating from 1873, owned by Charles Hooker Sn. The gears were held in by a strap
[C. E. Hooker

One of the steam gatherings the late Chris Lambert used to hold for his friends at Horsmonden. This one was on June 26, 1952
[J. H. Meredith

active imagination could conceive—the haulage of road materials, once road-making had ceased to be village responsibility, flour, potatoes, fertilisers (including night soil from towns with no or limited sewers, upon which task Jesse Ellis's Aveling was engaged when it blew up at Maidstone in 1880), household removals and even weddings. The author's friend Charles Hooker went to his wedding at St James, Church, Egerton, Kent behind an 1873 Aveling at Easter 1906. The interplay of horse and steam traffic is oddly illuminated by the recollection that in the days when there were half a million horses (civil and military) in London the late Chris Lambert of Horsmonden had two engines each with two traction wagons continuously employed on the haulage of stable manure from the railway siding to farms in the district, mainly for hop growers. It has always seemed ironic to the writer that the urban part of this idyll was the horse, where one would have expected a ready adoption of mechanical power and that in the depths of the Wealden countryside a progressive countryman used steam.

The truth of the matter is, however, that the traction engine belonged more to the country-

side than the town. A heavy preponderance of traction engine builders were countrymen. Thomas Aveling was a farmer turned engineer, Charles Burrell was a builder of agricultural machines as were Garrett of Leiston, Clayton & Shuttleworth, Ransomes, Wallis & Steevens, and Taskers. John Smith of Coven, early in the field with a traction engine, was a village blacksmith who progressed, whilst George Elston of Welby, Lincolnshire, who later built a solitary single-cylindered 2nhp engine, remained a blacksmith and village engineer throughout his life. John Fowler came to engine building, as was noted earlier in the chapter, by reason of his interest in steam ploughing and the standards in the works he established at Hunslet, Leeds in 1860 were heavily influenced by the railway engine building tradition already strongly entrenched in Leeds in the five firms of Fenton, Wood, Murray & Jackson; Kitson, Thompson & Hewitson; E. B. Wilson of the Railway Foundry; Manning, Wardle of the Boyne Engine Works, and Hudswell, Clarke & Co. Subsequently Leeds became a centre for builders of road steam engines harbouring besides Fowler's, the works of Mann & Charlesworth (later Mann's Patent Steam Cart and Wagon Company), Thomas Green & Sons, J. & H. McLaren, the Yorkshire Patent Steam

Wagon Company, and the Fisken Brothers, though not simultaneously. Kitson, Thompson & Hewitson had an even more direct influence on Fowler's standards of practice as the builders of certain of his ploughing engines constructed before he had sufficient capacity in his own works. That this influence was not only entirely good but also utterly urban is undoubted but despite it Fowler remained a countryman by birth and inclination.

Frederick Savage began in a small way as a blacksmith and founder at Kings Lynn whilst his fellow townsmen Alfred Dodman & Sons were general engineers and millwrights before making traction engines. Of all the firms who began building traction engines before 1870 and who saw the century out not one had its origin in the great industrial areas of Northumberland and Durham, Yorkshire, South Lancashire, the Black Country, South Wales or London. Many of these country firms built portable engines before they turned to traction work and the standards initially of many were undoubtedly crude. On the other hand the firms that remained in business after the mushroom builders had been eliminated, as most of them were by the time of the agricultural depression in 1879 at the latest, evolved a set of standards that were well suited to the work they were doing and to the class of customer to whom they were appealing. Burrell, Foden and Fowler and later, Foster, turned out workmanship that would stand comparison with that which emerged from the works of railway engine builders. Even the humble Wallis & Steevens engine which came in for a good deal of fun in its time—it was referred to as a "farmer's engine" or "blacksmith made"—was well suited to the buyers it went out to attract. It was indeed an engine for farmers or for the workman setting up for himself as a contractor. Deliberately kept simple and with refinements sparingly added because of the cost, it had corks in the hub oil fillers where dearer makes had filler tubes and screw caps, and a few blow holes did not disqualify castings provided their function was unimpaired. It was in consequence cheap to buy and, in the right hands, easy to manage and a good steamer, as a result of the use of $2\frac{1}{2}$in diameter boiler tubes where most makers did not exceed 2″ though it had a robust appetite. As well as being good steamers Wallis traction engine boilers seldom gave trouble from cracking in the flanges for, being largely formed up by hand, they were always worked at the proper degree of heat. Whilst a plate that had cooled could still be flanged on a hydraulic press by putting on more power it was not feasible to hand work a plate that had lost heat.

Though the traction engine is thought of as essentially a nineteenth century machine and it is true that the problems of its design were largely worked out before 1900, the numbers built up to that year were comparatively small. At the turn of the century Fowler had built about 9,000 engines, mainly ploughers and with a heavy emphasis on exports, Burrell about 1,800 and Avelings roughly the same. Marshall and Clayton & Shuttleworth, like Garrett, had reached very high works numbers because they had produced hordes of portable engines for the foreign markets but it is doubtful if the number of Marshall and Clayton traction engines together topped the 2,000 mark. Before 1900 many other makers including Tasker,

Two McLaren Colonials cooling down after a road test. The engine nearer the camera has about twenty-five pounds on the gauge

A traction engine of the middle period: Clayton & Shuttleworth No 23226 of 1886. Eight nhp, three shaft with an idler pinion on a stub shaft between the crankshaft and the countershaft. Claytons of this era were good engines for their time but the firm made the mistake of building the design for too long until it was completely outmoded [F. Gilford

Wallis & Steevens, Garrett, Hornsby, Dodman, and Savage were below the hundred in production figures for traction engines. It is by no means improbable that the total number of traction engines built in this country up to the end of the century—discounting ploughers and rollers—was hovering at about the 10,000 mark, a good part of which production had gone overseas. Since some allowance must be made for wastage it is thus quite likely that the home traction engine population was around 6,000, which meant that they were quite thinly spread over the country.

The upsurge in this country of the numbers of traction engines was brought about in part by the recovery of British agriculture from the depression that had lasted nearly twenty years from 1879, but it was given impetus by the provisions of the Locomotives on Highways Act of 1896 which not only relieved engines of the more onerous restrictions but imposed a uniform system throughout the country which very largely put engine owners out of the reach of the caprice of local boards and councils.

The Act of 1896 made possible for the first time the useful employment of light steam tractors and steam wagons. The latter are outside the scope of this book but the steam tractor was simply a very small traction engine. Under the 1896 Act tractors had to weigh not more than three tons unladen but a subsequent amending Act of 1903 revised this to five tons. The earlier restriction was so severe that few useful engines were built that complied —the five-ton limit was more practicable and led to the design and production of tractors in considerable numbers.

In theory there is no reason why a tractor should not be single cylindered and a few were produced in this form but for use at home the compound soon became the settled design, giving easier control in traffic, increased thermal efficiency and a quieter exhaust. The compound steam tractor became popular for a great variety of medium duty haulage. Ten tons could be handled with ease and loads of fifteen or sixteen tons were not unknown. Local authorities found the tractor a convenient method of hauling road materials, timber hauliers used them to take advantage of their higher speed and lighter weight, though as noted in the next chapter they had some limitations in this work, and a few were put to threshing. They also found their way on to the fairground, being a very convenient size for the lesser men and a useful tool for the larger proprietors to use for the minor tasks which were still done by horses and for what might be called colloquially "dodging about". The Garrett tractor, being somewhat bigger and heavier than most, was popular with showmen. Jacob Studt of Southampton bought No 26063 as early as May, 1907—the first of its line actually to be delivered to a customer for which he paid the penalty of having to see it through its teething troubles. John Studt of Cardiff had No 27185 in August, 1908 complete with dynamo and full showman's fittings though he kept it only for fourteen months after which it went to Mrs E. Smith while he had in its place No 27884 fitted with a colonial firebox. In 1909 Charles Hewson of Glasgow had No 27342 for his bioscope show and Tommy Cottrell of

Photograph taken in about 1895 of an Aveling & Porter single-cylinder road locomotive owned by Thomas Wood & Son of Crockenhill, Kent

[Thomas Wood & Son

Arthur Felgate's Robey single-cylinder traction engine at Vine Farm, Wivenhoe, Essex in 1905. The engine dated back to the early 'eighties but was an unimaginative design even for its time, notable in the unprotected gear train, the very small cast front wheels and the method of steering—analogous to that of the contemporary Aveling rollers

The Garrett "Suffolk Punch" tractor of 1917 was intended for direct ploughing as well as general farmwork

[Richard Garrett Engineering Works Ltd

Droitwich had No 31025 for the same purpose in 1913.

Another celebrated showman's Garrett is "Medina" new to James Humphreys of Pelsall, Staffordshire in August 1920 and still fortunately in preservation.

A typical tractor, such as the Aveling & Porter, would have cylinders of $4\frac{1}{2}$in $\times$ $6\frac{1}{2}$in bore by 9in stroke and would probably work at 200lb/sq in, would be provided with machine cut gears instead of gears dressed up from the black as in a traction engine, would have a belly tank to increase the range and would have covers on the motion and a solid flywheel. Such machines were marketed by all the well known builders of traction engines and several of the minor ones but a few firms struck out into new ground. Tasker of Andover produced the "Little Giant" in both a gear driven and a chain driven form whilst Foden launched a line of chain driven tractors based upon its design

Garrett No 4 tractor No 31632 of 1913 in use by Rose & Son of Kings Lynn

[R. G. Pratt collection

Garrett three-ton tractor No 25399 on trial by Carr Bros, Ipswich. Three-ton tractors were generally too small to be effective tools

of steam wagon, an example followed so slavishly by Nayler of Hereford that the latter was brought to heel on patent infringement, and more independently by Robeys of Lincoln. The process of devolution finally led to the vertical-boilered tractors of Sentinel and Atkinson which are outside the present scope.

Tractors reached the peak of their popularity about the end of World War I, production tapering off during the 1920s until the Salter report and the heavy taxation that followed it put an end to tractor building by about 1932. The building of agricultural traction engines continued until the mid-thirties on a reduced scale and outlived the steam tractor.

A Garrett No 5 single-cylinder Continental-type traction engine in use in France circa 1913

Chris Thompson's McLaren Miracle *at Apperley Bridge in May 1936*

[Cyclist

CHAPTER 2

The Traction Engine at Work

"I belong to a different system,
I belong to a byegone day".
The Passing of the Steam Locomotive.
J. Collopy.

THROUGHOUT the working life of the traction engine from beginning to end, its foremost employment was threshing. Other important tasks were performed but for the whole duration of the century of traction engines it was the work of separating the grain from the ear that gave makers the basic market for their products. Of the roots from which the traction engine came, the portable engine and thresher, which led to the self-moving portable and so on to the true traction engine, were probably the most fundamental.

The use of the portable threshing machine, known to generations of the threshing men as "the drum" or, less often "the box" or, in the Border and Scotland as "the mill", ante-dated the arrival of the self-moving engine by ten years or so but it is worth going back to the beginning of its use to trace the reasons for its importance. A 54in threshing drum of the 1850s could deal in a ten-hour working day with some seventy to eighty hundredweight of corn. The actual figure was regulated by the weight of corn in the straw, since the volume of straw fixed the capacity of the drum, and by the capabilities of the feeder and bond cutter, but 75cwt is near enough for this purpose. The yield of the best agricultural land at the time rarely exceeded and seldom equalled 35 bushels to the acre whilst the average was nearer 25 bushels. At 63lb to the bushel the crop off 300 arable acres would weigh, at 35 bushels to

the acre, only 5,906cwt, or about 80 days threshing.

The limited use of a thresher even on a very large arable acreage is thus apparent. In English farming practice, moreover, it is unusual to find anything like as much as 300 acres under corn on one farm, fifty being more common. Though a farmer could find other employment for a portable engine in cake crushing, grinding or chaff-cutting, a smaller engine than the eight or ten horse power engine used for threshing was quite suitable for these ancillary duties. Thus it became the accepted practice for one portable threshing set to serve several farms, either by the formation of a partnership or threshing company by the farmers concerned or by one of them or an outsider, purchasing the set and acting as a contractor.

Once contracting was established as a practice the immobility of the common portable became a distinct disadvantage for the owner had either to maintain his own team of draught horses in very intermittent employment or else to arrange for draught by the customer, possibly at a time when the latter needed his horses himself. The self-moving set when it evolved therefore met a growing commercial need and created a pattern that endured for virtually a century. However, contracting did not completely banish the portables from threshing; some continued in use well into this century.

A typical latter day contractor's outfit was made up of a 54in drum, a trusser, an elevator and, more rarely, a chaff cutter and, of course, the engine. The characteristic engine of the early years of threshing was an 8nhp, single or double-cylindered according to the owner's preference. As boiler pressures increased and the effective power output in relation to the nominal horsepower increased the 7nhp engine became popular, big enough to be capable but not so big as to be awkward in the average softish stackyard and often not too large for the constricted yards of the West Country or the extreme North West of England. In both these areas, the steam tractor later came into wide use because of its small size and light weight. On the other hand in the large hard yards of South Derbyshire and Nottinghamshire where any weight of engine was in order the contractors used eight and even ten horsepower engines, often compound, and quite frequently in retirement from road haulage or showground use.

Singles predominated in threshing. Compounds cost more initially and did not govern so well at lower pressures. A single would run quite nicely at eighty or 90lb pressure of steam but a compound was out of the question at less than about 140lb which difference in terms of steam raising time meant another twenty minutes or so, apart from the additional oiling time and cleaning required by the compound. Steam tractors required more driving than tractions, either singles or compounds. Single cylinder tractors never amounted to more than a handful and are therefore not really worth considering. Compound tractors of 4 or 5 nominal horsepower could, and did, run a 54in drum very well—as well in fact, if carefully handled, as a six horsepower engine and probably on rather less coal but, there were a number of disadvantages as well. With a smaller firebox they needed a rather better grade of coal, difficult sometimes to get when the customer was providing it and, since the same power had to be put through the belt, they had

A Burrell singlecrank compound owned by Lott & Walne, Dorchester, with a load of agricultural implements outside its owners' works and foundry at Fordington, Dorchester. The engine is a 6nhp and is either No 1764 or 2078—Lott & Walne owned both. From dress and other internal evidence the date would be about 1905

[R. G. Pratt collection

A photograph by the late Major Ind of a theshing train headed by an early Fowler traction engine complete with spring balance valves covered by the device known to the polite as the coffee pot and by the bawdy as a domestic pot of another kind

[R. G. Pratt collection

to run rather faster to give the right output resulting in a quick exhaust beat and a very bright hot fire that clinkered quickly. Whereas with a big old single cylinder traction the driver could fire up heavily, set the pump, wedge open the damper on the ashpan to just the right aperture with a piece of coal and leave the engine to itself for twenty minutes or half an hour whilst he attended to the corn sacks or did some other supplementary task to earn himself a few extra shillings, the tractor would not tolerate such treatment. It required firing little and often and, as the boiler was small, careful watching of the gauge glass to keep the level just right, otherwise there was a drop in pressure and a consequent slowing down of the drum.

In between the 7hp and the tractor came the 6hp engine, with a higher working pressure, usually either 160lb for a single or 180lb for a compound. Again the faults of the smaller engine working harder began to appear for though coal was undoubtedly saved the driver

had to be more attentive to avoid irregular performance.

The seven horsepower engine thus became a very convenient all-purpose engine, rather shorter, by twelve inches or so, than an eight and good for threshing and chaff cutting simultaneously. A foot in length sounds a trivial thing. In fact it could often make all the difference between being able to set up the tackle in a yard or not.

Threshing was always dusty work. Dust was shaken from the sheaves from the moment they were lifted off the stack to the time the eviscerated straw emerged from the shakers. With a brisk wind in the wrong direction a steady stream of debris could be blown over the engine to the extent that it could be impossible to look towards the machine without the eyes being filled with particles. If it did not enter the eyes it was sure to find its way round the neck and

Threshing when the sun shines. A Garrett tractor caught when the sun was high and the shadows intense

[R. G. Pratt

up the sleeves to produce a state of prickly discomfort.

All suffered from this nuisance—pitchers, bond cutters, feeder, sackman and the poor soul whose job it was to keep the bottom of the thresher free, raking over the caving sieve and seeing the straw fed into the tier and elevator. The men building the straw stack fared best— most of the dust and rubbish had gone by the time the straw reached them and they never suffered from the danger of rats or mice running up the inside of a trouser leg, to guard against which the men on the corn stack and on the ground would tie a thong around their trouser legs below the knees. Nevertheless, when the breeze was not tormenting the engine driver it might well be blowing across the straw stack so that those on it did not always escape.

The worst job connected with threshing, however, was that of feeding the straw from the shakers into the trough of the chaff cutter when one was used. When it was, there was no question of using anything less than a seven horsepower engine and an eight was better. The use of a chaff cutter practically doubled the load on the engine meaning that it was fully ex- tended for most of the time, a state of affairs reflected in the sharp increase in coal consump- tion. A daily ration of five to 6cwt would go up to the half ton mark or over. No longer was there any question of the driver doing the sacking for when he was not firing or coal breaking he was kept busy sharpening the spare cutter knives.

It has never seemed to the author that the chaff cutter was a well designed machine if a generalisation may be permitted on the various makes available. Basically the chaff was taken from the cutting wheel to the delivery point, either bin or bags, through some 15ft of sheet iron duct seldom more than 9in in diameter, by the blast of an impeller fan taking its drive from a secondary belt and running at double the speed of the drum. If the pace was being forced on the drum—and to earn a living it had to be fed as hard as possible—then it was all the

cutter fan could do to blow the chaff through the pipe. Everything ran on plain bearings which, with the rapid rotation and liberal dusting, always had a tendency to heat, the inevitable battering the pipe sustained did not help the flow of chaff and it needed only a patch of damp straw or a slight slackening of the fan belt to produce a stoppage resulting not only in an irritating delay but a most uncom- fortable job of dismantling and unstopping. If the straw feeder felt damp straw coming through he could, of course, throw some out to lessen the volume passing through but this feeding was such a shockingly uncomfortable job that mostly only the slow-witted or the desperate would do it and neither was calculated to be very selective in what he fed into the machine.

The procedure in threshing followed a set pattern. On arrival at the stack yard the set foreman, almost invariably the driver, would be shown or would select the first stack to be threshed and would draw the drum up to it. The drum was levelled with the jacks and chocked up, the shutters let down to make the feeding platform and the elevator placed in position. The driver would then run the engine round to the other end of the drum and set it to it, eyeing along the face of the flywheel on to the drum pulley. If the ground was reason- ably level all was well but an awkward slope needed to be corrected with a board or two.

Meanwhile the mate would run out the main band placing it on the drum pulley first and then on the flywheel. If the belt was too slack he would ask the driver to ease back and a prudent man would slip off the band whilst this was done, though sometimes to save time crews took a chance by leaving it on and hoping the driver really would set back six inches and not two feet with the resultant snatch on the drum and the probability of bending the drum spindle, damaging a bearing or simply upsetting the levelling of the drum. Once the belt was on the driver would put the engine out of gear and run it a few revolutions to ensure the belt was

A threshing outfit lined up in readiness to move off. The place and date are not known beyond that it was in Suffolk early in this century. The engine is a Burrell single. Of interest is the dress of the gang and the piling of straw on top of the drum to give a convex surface to the sheet so as to throw off the rain

[R. G. Pratt collection]

running true after which the governor belt would be put on.

Meanwhile the farm men would have had the thatch off the stack and tossed out any damp sheaves from the top. These usually went into the chicken run. The foreman would check the secondary belts, see the elevator belt on right, and give a turn on the stauffers, if the bearings ran in grease, or oil up if they did not, after which a final glance at the fire and gauge glass left the set ready for work.

The thresher was set in motion—a few turns slowly and then at the governed speed—and as soon as it was evident that all was running sweetly the pitchers would toss the first sheaf to the cutter who would cut and remove the binder twine and pass it to the feeder who, in his turn, distributed it on to the feed apron. As

it reached the concave, the sound of the idling drum settled down to the steady hum of the working machine, dust began to emerge from the cracks and a trickle of corn from the corn spouts. The beat of the engine came to a steady pattern and the outfit was at work in which state it would continue until the break for a bit of snap about nine o'clock.

The pitching was easy at first whilst the stack was high but as the day wore on and the stack diminished it got harder and dirtier—dirtier because it meant pitching overhead and harder from the height to which the sheaves had to be pitched. The curse of cutter and feeder was thistles. To cut the bonds and feed the sheaves into the drum without gloves could be very painful—to say the least.

As the stack was lowered the concentration

of rodents in it increased. A few made a bolt for it, braving the terriers but mostly the rats stayed in the bottom of the stack. Finally the nets were brought out and set up round the base with plenty of dogs and helpers in attendance as the last sheaves were cleared— then there was a slaughter of rats but however thorough the preparations some always got away.

Threshing men on the whole never really favoured the sprung engine just as they never wholly took to the compound. Both statements are offered with some diffidence as many sprung engines were in fact used just as were compounds. Springs added weight as well as initial cost and though they undoubtedly contributed to comfort on hard roads—which were, after all, relatively uncommon in the years up to 1914—

A winter threshing scene in Suffolk, probably in the late 'twenties. The engine is a Burrell, not otherwise identified. The screens are up on the drum to keep off the wind

[R. G. Pratt collection

Mann & Charlesworth 6hp three-shaft engine threshing in 1944 when owned by John Croft, Naburn, Yorks. The drum is less rare—made by Fosters of Lincoln, it was of a make less plentiful than Marshall or Clayton

[J. P. Mullett

Three-shaft Fowler threshing with a Marshall drum at Malton, Yorks in 1880. Note the method of straking the rear wheels in an effort to satisfy the Locomotive Act, 1865

[J. W. Pierson collection

Charles Cotton threshing at Hill Farm, Tuddenham, Suffolk in 1906. Henry Cotton is driving and Philip Cotton is cutting the bands. The engine is a single-cylinder Burrell

[R. G. Pratt collection

Threshing as the driver liked it—warm enough for shirt-sleeves, hard underfoot, and the smoke beating towards the drum. The engine is a Ransomes

Tuxford traction belonging to John Thorold of Syston threshing. This was Tuxford's answer to the problem of arranging steerage from the manstand—placing the driving wheels at the smokebox end

36

they did so at the expense of unsteadiness in traversing soft ground and increased rock whilst working on the belt. Some Wallis & Steevens sprung engines had a device for locking the springs whilst working on the belt. Where, however, an owner intended to use his traction engine for relatively long stints on the road, as, for instance, when an engine filled in the summer "off-season" of threshing by undertaking stone-haulage both springs and compounding paid. No one who has not endured the spine jarring motion of an unsprung engine over a hard road at anything in excess of some two miles per hour can appreciate the immeasurable relief that even the limited spring travel—perhaps $\frac{3}{8}$in or so—on a Wallis & Steevens or Garrett traction can give, whilst more sophisticated springing systems like those of the Foden, Fowler or Burrell seemed almost luxurious.

A side-task of the traction engine, sometimes but not invariably carried out at the same time as threshing, that has not survived the demise of the engine as a working force, was high density baling. Practically all baling now done is pick-up baling which produces very lightly compressed bales, easy to handle but regrettably difficult to load in commercially acceptable quantities on to road or rail transport, simply because the bulk to weight ratio of the bales is so high as to make almost laughable the weight that it is possible to pack on to even a large vehicle. The pick-up bale is handy for use on the farm but useless for transporting long distances and its emergence has lost the straw producer many of his more distant markets. In steam days, provided that there was enough yard space and engine power, a high density baler could be added to the threshing drum to receive the straw as it came from the shakers.

In the same way grass or clover crops that had been passed through a seeder could be baled up for storage or sale. Again hay was sometimes made into high density bales as it was carted. Without doubt the vast numbers of work horses in all the major cities of the country

A picture of J. P. Charter's Fowell No 93 at work threshing. Undated but about the turn of the century

Fowell (probably No 52) 8nhp owned by Percy E. Elbourn of Meldreth, Cambs, in a typical threshing scene

Burrell No 1679 (6hp single-crank compound) built in 1893. The picture is thought to date from the early 'twenties when the engine was owned by Henry Hammond, of Braconash, Norfolk
[R. G. Pratt collection

A high density baler at work powered by its owner's Fowell

A better life than the Western Front. Military baling teams on the road in the heat of a summer day during World War I

Foster No 2163 of 8nhp, owned by F. H. Cooke of Spalding, haymaking at Tongue End, Deeping Fen, a relatively unusual task for a traction engine. The engine is now owned by T. B. Paisley, and has Starke valve gear, a type of radial gear

The aim of many traction engine builders, achieved at best only partially—to design a steam tractor light enough to do direct traction ploughing on an English farm. The prototype Garrett Suffolk Punch on test in the late summer of 1917, probably on one of Lord Rayleigh's farms [Richard Garrett Engineering Works Ltd

A Burrell 5nhp owned by Darby & Son, Sutton, Cambs., hauling sugar beet. Harold Darby, the driver, is leaning on the belly tank. The engine is one of a series built for the War Department and all originally had cranes on the smokebox [H. Darby

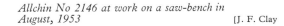

Allchin No 2146 at work on a saw-bench in August, 1953 [J. F. Clay

accounted for a large part of the market in baled fodder and bedding besides which there were the demands of the home based cavalry regiments, the artillery and the commissariat, all using horses. It was estimated that in 1899 the number of horses employed in London alone was 400,000* whilst the Army had some 500,000 horses. The outbreak of World War I intensified the demand for baled fodder for use by the enlarged army at home and in France. The demand was met at first by the use of civilian contractors but subsequently Army baling teams were used employing either engines

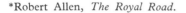

*Robert Allen, *The Royal Road.*

A military baling outfit, seemingly working better than most, complete with military driver and land girl, seen at Alwalton, Hants, late in World War I. The engine is a Ransome

The end of many a threshing firm. Thompson's two Fowells and three Wallis & Steevens lined up for sale at Upwood. In many cases their destination was the scrapyard

A very old photograph of an 1869 Burrell chain engine owned by Ballam of Mutton Hall, Wethersden, Suffolk, threshing in King's Field, Cross Street, Elmswell

[Suffolk Photo Survey

requisitioned from contractors or bought new from the makers. Baden Parsons related how his father's Burrell *Cornishman* was requisitioned by an Army impressing officer; "We are taking your engine now and we shall soon have your sons". On the whole the Army baling teams were not well managed. Professional engine men who volunteered or were conscripted were sent to the trenches whilst engines were sent out in the charge of half trained men quite unable to manage them competently, to set them to the baler or generally to get an adequate day's work out of them. The better type of men quickly improved but some remained ignorant hobble-de-hoys to the end, bullying other road users and lording it over their civilian helpers, including land-girls.

The war also led to a large increase in the use of steam in the timber trade both for extracting timber from the woods and converting it after extraction. The steam traction engine had had a long association with timber hauling, going

back to at least as far as the historic journey of the Burrell—Boydell from Thetford to Woolwich Arsenal in 1857 when one item of the load was a laden timber carriage. Timber work fell readily into the categories of extraction and conversion but extraction in turn could be classified into the three aspects of felling, removal from the wood and haulage from wood to mill.

So far as the actual felling was concerned the engine's part was limited. Tree-fellers could normally drop a tree where they wanted it without help but on occasion the assistance of an engine might be required as, for instance, when the falling tree might imperil a building or road or drop into a river or pond. Assistance was needed also when an ash or walnut tree with root burrs was to be taken out complete

The Fowler stump-puller. Designed with a very heavy strong rope drum with a slow drive, it had in addition a stronger rear axle and a special arrangement of the fair-leads

[B. J. Finch

for use by the veneer maker. This operation could be quite laborious, for to avoid damage to the burrs, it was necessary to excavate round the root of the tree and to cut off the roots as far as possible before attempting its removal. A further aspect of this sort of work was stump pulling, necessary where a tract had to be cleared not only of trees but also of the roots and stumps. Ordinary traction engines did this work using their roping drums and wire ropes, though Fowlers built a special stump pulling engine, suitably enlarged in the winding drum and associated parts and with additional fair leads. The engines that came off best in the matter of wire-roping were those such as the Wallis and Steevens where the drum was directly driven and the differential did not come into play during roping for this produced excessive wear besides overspeeding the drum and reducing the available power on the rope.

Apart from the exceptional occasions noted before, the extraction of the felled trees from the wood was normally the first and, in many ways, the most exacting of the jobs performed by the timberman's engine. The actual loading of the trees needed to be carried out on a reasonably level area, preferably firm under foot and clear of old stumps. A surprising number of the trees bought by sawmillers came from open fields or quite small copses where, by standing the engine at the edge of the copse, it was possible to rope out the felled trees to the open ground. In really deep woods, how-ever, this was out of the question and either the engine or horses had to go into the wood after the trees. A team of horses working in a wood was a wonderful sight to any but those with a feeling for horses—it was killing work for horses who sustained barked knees, broken limbs, and overstrain as well as respiratory troubles caused by spells of very heavy work alternating with waiting in idleness. In just the same way a traction engine or tractor in wood-land took a savage battering.

A big tree could well weigh up to twelve tons and to get such a log five hundred yards to the loading point through a wood in the wet months was a forbidding task. A steel shod engine was virtually inevitable and the paddles had to be on. Sometimes it might be possible to haul the log by direct traction by means of a chain round the butt carried to the engine drawbar but nine times out of any ten wire roping was necessary. In an extreme case the crew would have to anchor down the engine—the common method of doing which was to chain the front end to a tree and to place two five or six foot baulks with their butt ends on the ground and the other ends laid under a paddle so that when the pull was taken the paddles pulled down on to the top of the baulks and thus obliquely on to the ground—run out the rope to the felled tree and pull it up as near as was convenient to the engine. The engine would then be run forward seventy yards or so and the process repeated. The running forward might, in the very worst conditions, be accomplished only by winding the engine forward on the rope, making the whole process even more laborious.

The apotheosis of hard work came when the tree was too big or the terrain too rough to per-mit the use of single rope and the rope had to be run double through a snatch block. This halved the speed of travel at the same time as it halved the length of each pull, reducing the whole progression to an aching slowness.

Most tractors—the Garrett No 4 CD was the notable exception— carried only 50yds of rope on their drums whereas traction engines had seventy as did the Garrett tractor. Most makes of tractors were sent out with $\frac{1}{2}$in ropes though timber haulers frequently used $\frac{5}{8}$in for all replacements, thereby reducing the capacity of the drum further. The $\frac{5}{8}$in rope was virtually standard for traction engines. For the rough work off the road an unsprung traction, com-pound for preference to give the added ad-vantage of the double high for starting, was the ideal, followed by the steel-tyred tractor, with the rubber-tyred tractor almost a non-starter. Springs were just as much a nuisance in timber hauling as threshing.

A sequence of five stages in the extraction and loading of an oak log of some ten tons weight by a Garrett superheater tractor owned by the Express Motor Transport Co of Pershore, Worcestershire.
The engine was being demonstrated in 1919 to Lancaster Bros of Newent, Glos., who subsequently bought a Garrett

When the size of the firm and of the job permitted it was best to use a rigid traction in the field or wood and a rubber-shod tractor on the road and this was often done. Many an old traction engine spent its final year or two in this way until the differential bevels wore down to nothing, the intensive use joining with the presence of plenty of mud to wear them out in a tenth of their normal life. Old tractors were used up in the same way.

Few makers settled seriously to the task of making a powerful steam tractor specifically designed for the task with a separate winch and plenty of rope. Foden, Sentinel and Garrett did evolve designs for the job but they were derived more from steam wagon practice than from the traction engine and must await treatment on some future occasion.

One last aspect of the wire-roping process needs mention before passing on to loading and road work—the paying out of the rope. When the engine was fitted, as, for instance, was the Fowler, with a drum that could be fast or loose at will it meant that the rope could be run out as the engine was drawn forward. If the drum was fast on the axle as it generally was then the rope had to be pulled back to the starting point after the driving pin had been taken from the engine wheel and the engine had been reversed —not too bad a job if there was a horse to help but hard work if it had to be done by the mate.

Loading was done up skids. The timber tug was set in a clearing and the log drawn up beside and parallel to it, ten to twelve feet distant. Stout ash or chestnut skids, roughly squared one end to lay easily on the bolsters or to suit the sockets on the bolsters of the tug, where these were fitted, were set up from the ground to the bolsters to make the ramp up which the log would roll. The engine was then placed at right angles to the tug, back to it and on the opposite side to the log. Two long chains were run from the skids round the centre pole of the tug just on the inward side of each bolster, passing under each end of the log and back over it and over the tug to the hook on the end of the engine's wire rope. The placing of the tug in relation to the log and the chains in relation to both called for considerable skill, of the loader rather than the driver. The engine was then run gently until the slack rope and chain was taken up after which, taking his cue from the loader's hand signals the driver would give more steam until the tree trunk was rolled up to the skids. If it was moving into position nicely the pull might be continued with increasing power until it was rolled up on to the bolsters of the tug but if it was coming awkwardly there would be a pause for adjustments. With a straight tree and well positioned chains the whole job could take a few minutes but if the shape of the tree was awkward it could take up to an hour to load.

Once it was on it was chained down to the bolsters, tightening bats of ash were twisted into the chains and were themselves secured by chaining the free end to the centre pole. The load was now ready for getting on to the road, a task sometimes possible by simply coupling the tractor up to the tug and moving off but more often requiring further wire-roping— first perhaps to get the tractor itself on to the road and subsequently to get the laden tug out after it. Because of the narrowness of so many country roads it was often necessary to pull the tug at right angles to the public road, which required a snatch block opposite the gateway to take the wire rope. To give an oblique angle of travel to the front wheels of the tug the rope would be fixed to the nearside or offside, as required, of the forecarriage and the steering angle adjusted by a sling-off chain from the draw eye of the tug to the haulage rope.

The author's friends, the Newells of Westerham, Kent, were a family of father and two sons who earned a living by owning and working a timber haulage business. Bill, the surviving brother, was going through a wire-roping exercise near Horsmonden some thirty-eight years ago, in which he had to rope his tractor, an Aveling Colonial, together with the laden timber tug off a soft woodland road up a slope and over the lip of the hard public road. To do this the rope was put out across the road and chained to a growing tree. The engine had reached the very edge of the hard road when the rope broke. In consequence, complete with load, it ran back into the wood, crashing over the stumps of felled trees and underwood until it came to rest with the engine embedded so deeply that it was resting on the bottom of the tank and ashpan. A few minutes' inspection after Bill had recovered himself and his brother, Jack, and his father, Tom, had run back into the wood showed that the adjusting nut of the spring had been knocked off by one of the passing tree stumps. Fortunately an appeal to

Land clearance by steam. Gordon Lugg and his late father, James Lugg, on leading and second engine respectively working with their single-cylinder Fowler ploughers

Another Wallis oilbath tractor owned by A. Knowlton, a timber merchant of Weybridge, Surrey, hauling wood from the tops of trees. Engine No 7480 (AA5467)

A Mann & Charlesworth 5-ton tractor rolling up timber in May 1916 on the Aldenham Estate, Hertfordshire. The engine is No 1017 (U3843), owned by Lord Aldenham

The same Mann & Charlesworth engine (opposite) and load ready for the road

Sawmilling in the wood. A rack with what appears to be a Marshall portable. The guard on the driving belt is a contrast to the unguarded belts in the threshing scenes. Sawmills were subject to the Factories Acts—agricultural contractors were not. The owners were G & A Wright of Blyth. The scene was at Little Ryal, Northumberland in 1937

[Dr. J. Middlemiss collection

The woodland sawmill from another angle—hauling the log trolley up the temporary railway by means of the tractor and snatch-block. The tractor is a Burrell showman's   Dr. J. Middlemiss collection

the late Chris Lambert of Horsmonden produced help in the shape of a 6hp traction engine which was able to extricate both the damaged tractor and its load.

The same family—or at least Tom and Jack, for Bill was on the road at the time with his Aveling—were involved in another accident that, though it caused no bodily injury, might have done. This happened at Manor Farm, Sundridge, not far from their home town of Westerham where they were extracting trees from a hill-top wood downhill through an orchard at the foot of which the track turned at right angles along the bank of a stream. When wet the track was as greasy as a skid patch and to give better control they were in the habit of dragging a log on a chain behind the laden timber tug. On the wet day in question this trailing log hit an apple tree and broke the chain. Jack, who was driving the Garrett tractor, was now really in trouble. If he braked the tractor either it had no effect or, if it did, the load began to jack knife. He came on through the orchard steering by luck or extreme skill, between the trees till he reached the right angle. Here the choice was agonising. If he went on the tractor would plunge into the stream with the laden tug on top of it whilst if he took the turn the weight of the tug would almost as certainly push it over. As the lesser evil he chose the latter. The tractor was, predictably, pushed over and the driver lifted sharply through the match boarded and felted roof, subsequently sitting up bruised but not otherwise hurt on the river bank. The tractor was a sad sight with chimney and cab smashed and the rear axle bent and as Tom ran down through the orchard to the scene of the accident he could picture Jack trapped underneath, for he was nowhere in view. Tom scrabbled under

the engine amid the spilled coal and the escaping steam.

"Where are you, Jack, where are you?" he shouted.

Jack got to his feet a little unsteadily, walked round behind his father and remarked, "If you're looking for me I'm over here."

Seldom could two difficult characters have been so pleased to see one another. When Bill

In the forests of Oregon about the turn of the century. An engine built in 1894 by the Best Manufacturing Co of San Leandro, California—one of the few American makers to concentrate on engines for heavy haulage
[Hal Higgins collection, University of California

McLaren compound hauling pit timber during World War I. The first truck has gained a somewhat odd pair of rear wheels

returned with the Aveling they pulled the Garrett back on to its wheels, jammed the broken chimney into the stump, hacked off the remains of the cab and put it back to work. The bent axle was never repaired and the engine spent its few remaining years with a distinctly wobbling gait.

On the hard high road, haulage was not so bad though in the middle of winter when it was dark by mid-afternoon, lights became a problem. Two hurricane lamps on the front axle were the favourite illumination with a similar lamp having a ruby glass on the end of the longest tree though there were, of course, numerous makes of tractor lamp on the market. Lamps, however, had a poor life expectancy in timber hauling and the common hurricane was the cheapest to replace as well as being surprisingly efficient.

The other task performed by steam engines in the wood was sawing, either conversion of round timber into planks and quartering or of underwood and coppice timber into pit timbers. Saw benches were being offered by the makers of traction engines from the very beginning and portable rack benches were offered at least as early as the mid-eighties. So far as this country is concerned the bulk of the timber converted in the woods was what was sometimes known as "estate" material, suitable for fence and gate posts, farm buildings and gates and similar rough use but not for the best class of work,

being converted from the tops and major limbs of large trees and from coppice trees rather than prime butts. Pit timbers were not an important item of rural commerce until World War I when the demand for timbers to be used in the trenches and dugouts of the Western front and the need for increased numbers of props for collieries because of extra coal production put a strain upon supplies from abroad at a time when shipping was under attack by the German navy. Trees were felled in large numbers in the New Forest, in Ashdown Forest, in Windsor Great Park and in Wales and the Border counties and in lesser quantities on innumerable estates and woodlands up and down the country. Traction engines and tractors were the only effective agents for carrying the props over rough terrain though part of the work of hauling them on the road to the railway stations was taken by steam wagons, a smaller part by horses and a minute quantity by motor lorry. It has been estimated that in 1918 five million tons of pit and trench timber were produced in Great Britain so the extent of the job can be gauged from that.

This brings in the whole matter of road haulage by traction engine, a subject going back to the 'fifties and 'sixties of the last century. By about 1860 most of the country was effectively served by the main lines of railways, the trunk lines subsequently built being either, as in the case of the Manchester, Sheffield & Lincolnshire's line to London, which turned it into the Great Central in 1899, an attempt to compete with other lines or, as with the Great Western's Westbury cut-off (1901) an effort to improve running and timing over existing routes. The shipping of the coast and rivers carried appreciable quantities of goods where it could reach whilst canals retained some of their once heavy

An Aveling and Porter 6nhp single-cylinder traction engine at Westleton, Suffolk, in March 1899. The owner was G. R. Le Grys of Heveningham. He had three engines of this type, more or less identical, but subsequently he became a customer of Garrett nearby, whose prototype clover huller was tried on his farm in 1896

[R. G. Pratt collection

traffic, but in the main, the country slid into an almost total reliance upon railways for transport over distances exceeding eight to ten miles. The life of rural communities was local in the extreme for the effective capacity of a horse in a day was not more than about twenty-five miles and where no rail facilities existed such a simple thing as a family party might mean some weeks of preparation with overnight accommodation for guests who lived beyond the daily range of the horse. This was reflected again in the local nature of everyday supplies. Every town and many a large village had at least one brewery, millers and corn merchants were equally common, whilst surprisingly, mineral water manufacturers were, if anything, more plentiful then brewers, though the volume of their products was less. In the author's own small area of the Weald there were breweries at Tunbridge Wells (Kelsey), Frant (Ware & Sons), Lamberhurst (Smith), Hadlow (Kenward & Court), Tonbridge (two—Bartrup and Baker), Sevenoaks (two—Bligh and Golding), Westerham (Bushell), West Malling (Phillips), Wrotham (Golding), Yalding (Wickham) and Wateringbury (two—Jude Hanbury and Leney). Regrettably only one survives.

To transport even builders' sand or roadstone for ten miles by horse and cart was laborious so that materials at hand were used whenever possible. Many a builder's yard sported a portable or fixed engine coupled to a mortar pan so that old lime plaster, cinders or old soft bricks could be reground to make the aggregate for mortar whilst stones picked from the fields provided much of the road material. Perhaps this is why the Fens, having effectively no stones in their fields, came off so badly for roads. For short distance traffic in heavy or dirty materials the traction engine was brought into use almost at its first appearance and the designers of both the Bray and the Boydell engines had haulage primarily in view. Though repressive legislation discouraged effective development of long distance heavy haulage until the end of the nineteenth century, the traction engine as an agent for local cartage was well established by the 'eighties, carting sand, brick, stone, manure, flour and other heavy or bulky commodities associated with the life of the market towns and their rural hinterlands. For the greater part this need was supplied by ordinary agricultural traction engines, quite often doing the work in the summer off-season between the end of one year's threshing and the beginning of the next.

Change was at hand, however, in the legislative atmosphere. In part the mere operation of time was responsible, for death and retirement removed old diehards from the benches of magistrates, rural pulpits and vestry committees with grim inevitability to be replaced by men tempered by having lived only in the age of machinery. Mechanical invention in quite another field played its part also for the arrival of the bicycle upon the scene about 1870 was the signal for a rapid and popular development that progressed by way of the "ordinary" or "penny-farthing" to the safety bicycle that appeared in the beginning of the 'eighties, though reputed to have been invented by H. J. Lawson in 1876. As the cycle at a price of ten or twelve pounds was out of reach of most working men and of no particular attraction to the upper classes, for the first twenty years of its life it became the hobby of men from the newly enfranchised and highly articulate middle and lower middle classes—schoolmasters, shopkeepers, solicitor's clerks and other categories in the hundred pounds a year and upward brackets. From 1876 when "Bicycling News" first appeared to 1898 when there were twenty weekly papers covering cycling, the clamour of the cyclist for better roads grew more and more insistent till even the politicians heard it. The formation of county councils under the 1888 Act provided at length the mechanism for achieving their objective. Its relevance to the present account is that the trend to the improvement of roads led to the use of increasing numbers of steam rollers, a large increase in the consumption of

A street scene of the pre-motor age—the road locomotive and the horse as primer movers. The locomotive is a Fowler compound

road stones and the emergence, or more accurately the re-emergence, of road contractors. The only effective instrument for the extra carrying from wharf, rail-head or quarry was the traction engine and it would seem fair to infer that to this can be ascribed the change of atmosphere in central and local government circles that led to the Locomotives on Highways Act of 1896 which in its turn made steam road haulage practicable on a worthwhile scale. Heavy haulage by road had, on a circumscribed scale, ante-dated the 1896 Act. Firms such as Coupe Brothers of Sheffield had used traction engines for the local moving of exceptionally heavy ingots or machinery but the industry as known in this century began after 1896.

The fact that councils were themselves using steam rollers and traction engines led to a softening in the attitude of local government officers toward traction engines for even granted the nineteenth century official's apparently limitless capacity for self-deception it was scarcely possible to adopt the attitude of "do as I say and not as I do". Even so there were some remarkable cases of intransigence. Though most of the Lancashire industrial towns took a reasonably enlightened attitude to steam traction, Rochdale, despite its dependence on industry, seemed to set its corporate mind against it. Whilst, therefore, the adjacent boroughs confined steam traction to the hours of daylight Rochdale limited it to the night. Again it prohibited the use of more than one engine on a load. When the Town Clerk was asked by a contractor with a large indivisible load, requiring the efforts of two engines, how he suggested it be hauled through Rochdale he replied, says the report, "with a smile" that it would have to be taken some other way—under the impression, one would assume, that he had made a remark that was intelligent or witty.

Nevertheless the use of steam for local cartage began to increase as the century closed, partly by agricultural contractors using their engines for cartage work, partly by the new race of road contractors buying engines and again by the emergence of the steam haulage contractor as a distinct force. For a spell, the

Steam carriage of the 1860s by Cooke & Sons of York, from a contemporary photograph. One is left in doubt as to the method of communication between the steersman at the front and the driver at the rear

[F. D. Simpson collection

An unidentified McLaren, intended for export, photographed on test

Members of Haddenham (Bucks) Baptist Sunday School about to leave for a trip to Whiteleaf Cross (a local beauty spot near Princes Risborough). It was taken at Fort End, Haddenham, and the house in the background was the home of the owner of the engine, Mr B. R. Green. Several years after this picture was taken, Mr Green was run over and killed by the back wheels of this same engine

Foster tractor No 3057 owned by W. J. Lobjoit & Son, Heston, Middx. with a trailer by the same maker for hauling market garden produce to Covent Garden. An earlier use of converted horse wagons was not successful

Fowell hauling flour c. 1907. The leading wagon is lettered "W. L. Fletcher, Binbrook"

height of which the author would put at 1905-6, there was a vogue for the convertible roller which could be dressed either as a roller or a traction engine, the idea being that in the summer months it would haul stones and in the winter months roll them in. Apart from the laborious process of reversing the purpose twice a year this scheme had some success, albeit that a good roller made a very small traction engine or a sound traction engine an extremely heavy roller, until the arrival of tarred macadam, which had to be laid and rolled as soon as it was hauled, put an end to this arrangement. By the beginning of the 1914-18 War, few convertibles were undergoing their bi-annual metamorphosis—by the end of it their use had, for all practical purposes, vanished.

This bi-valence of the traction engine was expressed in another way, again arising from the seasonal traffic in stone. Whereas for time out of mind stone had been broken at the roadside by the stone-cracker in his gauze goggles, using the familiar hammer with the carefully selected hazel handle for resilience, the increased demand led to the use of power-operated stone crushers at the quarry. For a while, portables were the power source but they were joined by traction engines off-season and later still, in a few cases, by steam rollers fitted with governors, in their erstwhile idle period. It is easy, in generalising, to oversimplify the picture, for in fact the changes did not take place in concert or even in waves but in a kind of rash, wherever a surveyor or quarry owner was influenced by what he saw or read.

By the late 'nineties the advocates of road improvement, of which cyclists had hitherto been the mainstay, were reinforced by a new force—the motorists. Motoring tapped a new stratum of society so far as the movement towards superior roads was concerned, drawing most of its support from the affluent—a catholic mixture of merchants, manufacturers, stock-brokers and the titled. Road traffic began to be taken seriously at Westminster, where there had been a tendency hitherto to regard it rather as an annoyance.

A trade which seized eagerly upon this resurgence of road haulage was that of the furniture remover. The vehicle for moving furniture was the pantechnicon—a four-wheeled van with a low floor hauled by two, or more, horses. Vans of this description were used in London as late as the end of the 1940s and some, converted to pneumatic tyres, survived even longer as trailers to motor tractors, so well were they adapted to their purpose. Over long distances, however, they were terribly slow and the practice arose of despatching them by rail upon carriage trucks— a mixed blessing that gave the remover the choice of either sending them on continuously braked close-coupled vehicles by passenger or parcels trains, a high expense, or by loose coupled goods trains with the high risk of damage to the contents. The appeal of a prime mover that would enable his own vans to cover long journeys relatively fast without recourse to the railway is therefore apparent.

Furniture had, in fact, been steam hauled at irregular intervals ever since the first appearance of the traction engine but regular furniture bumping began in the latter 'nineties with such firms as Lalonde Brothers & Parham (using its

Furniture bumping just before World War I. Wallis & Steevens tractor, No 7480 with oilbath enclosing the motion, known to the irreverent as the fishfrier. *The vans belonged to Reeves and Co and the engine to Gadd of Wokingham*

own engines), Heelas of Reading (using Charles Openshaw's), Pickford, Rudd, Thorpe and a dozen or so other firms round the country. Furniture removers and storers who had no engines of their own hired them from local firms when needed. Since bulk rather than weight characterised a load of furniture, three pantechnicons and their loads, even of the heavy furniture from a country mansion, made a comparatively light load for an 8hp road engine. A 6hp, provided that its gear ratios and other appropriate characteristics were suitable, was considered the right size by many hauliers.

Lalonde Brothers & Parham, of Weston-super-Mare, whose engines and vans were seen in most parts of the country at one time or another, used 6hp Fowler road locomotives with considerable success but the considered opinion was, after several years of use, that the fireboxes needed to be a little longer—"one stay longer" was the actual phrase used—a suggestion not taken seriously at Hunslet. Lalonde Brothers rightly considered that as theirs was a serious comment, prompted by experience and reinforced by the willingness to pay for the extra cost, it had the right to proper examination. Legend, as preserved in the recollections of their staff, says that this was not forthcoming and that as a result of their rebuff from Fowler the partners took their problem to Richard Garrett & Sons with the result that the Garrett No 6, "Express", road locomotive was designed in 1908. It was indeed, known as the "Garrett-Lalonde" in its early days—until in fact the brief dalliance of Lalondes with Garrett came to an end. It ended because the realisation came to the Lalonde firm that the co-operative attitude at Leiston was no adequate substitute for Fowler's experience of road locomotive design and to Fowler that it had been over brusque with a valuable customer. Though the rapprochement is touching the real interest of the episode lies in the characteristics with which the Garrett No 6 was endowed—large wheels,

two gears—one fairly high, the other a hillclimber—geared down pump and large firebox. The actual design as built suffered from bearing trouble, a tendency to overheat, and from cracked crankshafts which fatigued at the centre point between the high pressure and low pressure crank webs, a trouble later alleviated by a fitted collar which bolted round the fragile part guarding it against the whipping which caused the metal fatigue and, incidentally, providing some improvement in the wear of the brasses which were relieved of the eccentric friction caused by the former flexing of the crankshaft.

Some of Lalonde's drivers made their high-steppers put their best foot forward. Tom Newell who later became a timber haulier as noted earlier in this chapter worked, as a young man, for Lalonde where he acquired the habit of what he described as "pushing on a bit." The late Roger Norton, of Headcorn, himself no sluggard, described the occasion when, descending River Hill on the present A.21 between Sevenoaks and Tonbridge with an engine and wagons, he was overtaken by Tom on another engine, out of gear, with two loads behind. The event was on the straight lower part of the hill, but even so the dexterity required to steer at that speed with chain and bobbin steering was considerable.

Though furniture removers saw plenty of the country and had their share of excitements the efforts required in moving the contents of a house were negligible compared to those required to transport the steam accumulator shewn on page 53, when every sharp corner was an adventure and every drain or culvert a hazard. Really heavy haulage abounded, in fact, in hazards. From 1858 when one of the Bray Traction engines hauling a 22-ton mainshaft from Penn's engineering works at Deptford to Woolwich Dockyard trod through the roadway in Nelson Street, Greenwich because of the collapse of cellars under the road, to 1936, almost at the end of heavy haulage by steam, when the famous accident with the Hackbridge transformers took place near Cobham, the occupation was an adventure.

We have looked at the reasons for the tendency of public and official opposition to the haulage engine to relax by the end of the last century but before heavy haulage by road became a reality a further factor was necessary —a demand. Very large heavy objects had already been transported locally by teams of horses or by traction engines for many years without a widespread trade in long distance haulage evolving, though isolated examples of this were performed from time to time. One of the social changes that triggered off an increase in road hauled traffic was the emergence of electricity generation as an important industry—in Tunbridge Wells, for instance, where in 1895 there were only 400 consumers, there were over 1,000 by 1900, a rate of growth reflected in other towns throughout the country, creating a demand for the transport of heavy pieces of machinery about the country. The new traffic was important to the road haulier because so much of it was out of gauge for the railway and consequently could be carried only by road. Ever since, electricity generation has provided the heavy haulage contractors with a substantial amount of work each year.

Four makers of engine were important in the heavy field—Fowler, Burrell, Foster and McLaren in that order, with Aveling & Porter a doubtful fifth* and all others virtually nowhere. The eight horsepower was the standard engine supplemented by a few tens and rather more sixes—virtually all compound and predominantly three speed. The vehicles used provided the diversity, ranging from the rock-bottom crudity of the traditional boiler maker's trolley, unsprung, on steel tyred wheels the size of shirt buttons, with plain bearings and a forecarriage so stiff under load as almost to defy direction, to the double bogie rubber-tyred well wagon, each bogie on two, occasionally

---

*The profitable trade in rollers overshadowed road locomotive development.

Garrett's works crane engine No 23021 caught about 1907 at the junction of Main Street and Gas Hill, Leiston. She was the only crane engine ever built at Leiston Works

three, axles with perhaps eight carrying wheels in line across the vehicle, and each bogie steering when necessary. Such vehicles began to come into use by the leading firms by about 1910 and were widely used by ten years later, the law finally abolishing the non-resilient tyred trolley in 1926. The last aspect of the heavy haulage business was the crane engine, either the road locomotive more or less permanently dressed for crane work with a jib at the smokebox end or the temporary crane engine using either a wheeled crane for attachment to the engine drawbar, or the tender-mounted crane, in each case the power being taken from the engine's winding drum.

A traction engine by a village engineer. Fyson No 1 built in 1894 at the village of Soham by C. J. R. Fyson (holding the child behind the engine). The gears on this engine were made by Fowell at St Ives. Seventeen Fyson traction engines were made, the last in May, 1924

[R. G. Pratt collection

The latter day trailers used in heavy haulage may fairly be said to be based upon the Fowler trailer built in 1927 on sixteen twin solid rubber-tyred wheels arranged in four bogies side by side in pairs, those at the rear end all braked. Though the overall length was 37ft, the actual well was 16ft long by 7ft 9in wide with a floor 2ft above the road. The designed load was stated to be 85 tons and the tare 30 tons—

Garrett tractor No 32622 Thor *owned by Southern Transport Ltd of Brighton hauling boiler house plant to Southwick power station, Sussex*

"Where every corner is an adventure". Fowler No 16263 Talisman *leading No 17105* Atlas *on the epic journey from Annan to Beckton in January, 1938. Both engines were then owned by Pickfords who had taken over the business of their former owner, Norman E. Box*

the latter was probably accurate but the former was undoubtedly a fairly nominal matter treated as a guide rather than a dictum.

The famous Fowler Super Lion No 17105 *Atlas* is on record as having, single-handed, transported from Annan to Glasgow a 90-ton steam accumulator which, with the trailer, must have made up a gross load of the order of 120 tons. Speed, of course, would have been very low—probably never more than 2½mph and often one or less and low wheel would have been used. Probably the most famous journey made by Pickford Super Lions was that in which another steam accumulator 70ft long and 12ft diameter was moved from Cochrane's at Annan to Beckton Gas Works, 325 miles, by three engines in 1938. This was widely reported and is said to have been, at the time, the world's largest indivisible load to date though not by any means the heaviest. The journey was started on January 6 and took twenty-one days, eighteen of which were actual travelling time. Snow caused delay over Shap but otherwise no particular troubles were encountered. Speed averaged 2mph outside London and, rather surprisingly, 3mph in the Metropolitan Police area, mainly because of three factors—the travelling in London was done at night, full police escort and traffic control were provided and use was made of a 3,000-gallon tank of boiler feed water over this section to avoid trouble with water. The trolley used was built by Crane of Dereham and consisted of two sixteen-wheeled bogies. The haulage was done by the ex-Box engines No 16263 *Talisman* and No 17105 *Ajax* with No 16264 *Jix** in attendance with the living van to provide braking or rear steerage as required.

A journey of this character demanded, apart from the sheer expertise of the men involved in the actual haulage, an enormous amount of preparatory work. A complete survey of the

*"Jix" was the nickname of William Joynson-Hicks—Norman Box's friend and legal adviser to the National Traction Engine Owners' and Users' Association.

route was made and rechecked a few days ahead of the actual journey. All bridge authorities were notified two days ahead of the passage of the load and certain bridges were shored up for its passage. Preparations for the Beckton journey began eighteen months before it actually took place and this was by no means an exceptionally long time. Another out of gauge load moved by the same firm and team a few weeks later required the temporary lowering of the roadway under a bridge in South Wales.

The dodges used by the hauliers to get round obstacles were innumerable and ingenious. The stock way of getting a long load round a right angled corner too narrow for it to follow its proper track was to run the rear wheels on to steel plates and then pull or push it bodily sideways. On one occasion Edward Box's Super Lion No 17106 did this with the Scammell hundred tonner laden with an 80-ton

Manchester heavy haulier Norman Box's Titan— *Fowler No 14843*
[Entwistle and Thorpe

Norman Box's Atlas *preparing to depart from Harland & Wolff's works single-handed with an RAF motor launch*
[Entwistle and Thorpe

Vulcan *(Fowler No 14844) and* Atlas *leaving the Metropolitan-Vickers works at Manchester*
[Entwistle and Thorpe

Garrett No 4 tractor No 32680 of 1915 owned by
Norman Box. The engine had Tangent rear wheels
built at the Tangent Wheel Works at Clapham,
afterwards owned by Baulys of Bow. The spokes
were set at a tangent to the centre so that when the
wheel was revolving forward the thrust tended to
send the spokes tighter in. The crude trolley is
typical of the time and the huge load for such a
small engine is characteristic of what Norman Box
expected of his tractors

[Richard Garrett Engineering Works Ltd

Norman Box's Talisman piloting Atlas on an
unspecified, but heavy, load after they had passed to
Pickford ownership

Talisman and Atlas in Norman Box partnership

girder. Tram or trolleybus overhead and its poles were two bugbears that added to the fun and on at least one occasion the Glasgow Corporation Tramways dismantled a section of overhead to allow William Kerr to take two massive marine boilers under it. Norman Box recalled (to W. J. Hughes) how he had caused the temporary removal and subsequent re-instatement of the gas lamp posts through the whole length of a village street. He also related on another occasion to Victor Garrett how he

The saga of the boiler. In 1924 a new boiler was delivered to the Royal Laundry, Brentwood, by Thomas W. Ward Ltd, from the company's depot at Silvertown. Brook Street Hill on the London side of Brentwood was too steep for the engine (Garrett No 4 tractor, works No 32740—1915). It was decided, therefore, to take the load up on the winding rope by stages anchoring the tractor to telegraph poles as it worked. The fact that the poles were on the south bound side of the road and the boiler was going north did not deter the gang.

Picture 1 shows the first stall, with the old Commer lorry that carried the packing attached to the front in an abortive attempt to haul the load up by direct traction. Pictures 2 and 3 show the warping in progress. Picture 4 shows the operation completed and the load on level ground again. The final picture shows the satisfied enginemen with the boiler finally coaxed into the laundry yard

[F.D. Simpson

The yard of Thomas Wood & Son, Crockenhill, Kent, towards the end of the days of steam. Note the engine on its side under the sheer legs for firebox repairs

[Thomas Wood & Son

used to haul, quite illegally, sixteen tons behind a Garrett No 4 compound tractor in the charge of one man.

Whatever subterfuges the heavy hauliers resorted to they were as nothing compared with the deeds of the showmen. Showground life and the way in which the showman's engine merged into it is a subject worthy of a long book in itself, and no more than a snatched look can be taken here. The haulage engine came seriously to the fairground about the early 'eighties—it would be outside the scope of this book to attempt to elucidate which showman was the first to use steam haulage or what he used. It came for the reason that other road users turned to it, namely the high cost and inconvenience of horse traction. Apart from the initial cost of a heavy draught horse the expense of feeding and maintaining it was also high, involving the keeping of separate horse-men who could not get fully involved in the work of the fair and who had, moreover, to be kept on, at least in part, whilst the show was in winter quarters and earning no money. However the master showmen were a relatively conservative crowd and the increase in the numbers of steam haulage engines would probably have taken place at a much slower rate had it not been for a second happening— the arrival of commercial electric lamps. The novelty value of electric light was enormous. E. H. Bostock, the menagerie proprietor who began illuminating his show by electricity generated by a portable engine and dynamo on November 3, 1890 wrote of it, "This was a great feature, quite a number of patrons coming to see it alone". The novelty of handling the portable engine and its dynamo truck on soft fields and poor roads soon wore off for the showmen. Two firms who built for the fair-ground, Thomas Green & Son of Leeds and Savages of Lynn each produced electric light engines, portable engines carrying, on the same truck, the dynamo to which they were belted,

which did abolish the tiresome labour of setting the portable engine to the dynamo but neverthe-less left the anomaly of six or so horses hauling a machine capable of producing a power output such that if applied to its wheels it would have propelled not only itself but a substantial load as well.

This state of affairs, which had so irked Thomas Aveling thirty years earlier, did not long persist to irritate the travellers. The advances in dynamo design consequent upon the work of Dr J. Hopkinson* and the sub-stitution of the carbon brush for the copper gauze brush placed on the market compact and relatively efficient generators which, by an extension of the reasoning that had prompted the electric light engine, were capable of being mounted upon a traction engine. After a short-lived experiment by Aveling & Porter with a dynamo mounted above the motion where it could be gear driven, the firm of Charles Burrell & Sons Ltd evolved the idea of the dynamo mounted upon a bracket in front of the chimney where it could be belt driven from the flywheel, a position from which it never deviated whilst engines continued to be built for showmen. The firm of Laurence Scott of Norwich was associated with Burrell in the supply of dynamos for use on certain early showmen's engines. Other firms that supplied early dynamos for mounting on road engines were Mather & Platt Ltd of Manchester, Baxendale of Manchester and Stevens of London.

The first engine supplied by Burrell to a showman and fitted with a dynamo by the firm was No 1451 *Monarch* built in 1889 for Jacob Studt, of Pontypridd—others may have been converted before. The twisted brass casings to the cab standards, the stars and rings, elaborate lining and lettering, the yellow or maroon wheels—said, though not by showmen,

---

*First set out in his paper "Dynamo-Electric Machinery", Phil. Trans. May 6, 1886, and elaborated in a second paper of the same title. Proc. Roy. Soc. February 15, 1892.

to denote whether the owner was of Romany or Irish descent—were absent from the first engine but were not long in appearing, being a natural projection of the methods of ornament applied to fairground furniture and particularly the rides.

Short cabs were soon superseded by the familiar extended awning reaching forward of the chimney to cover the dynamo. Singles were used in the early years of showmen's engines but were soon outnumbered by compounds, mainly double-cranked but with a few of Burrell's patent single crank compounds.

Fuel economy was a sufficient justification for the change though the inconvenience of starting a single under load if the driver had had the misfortune to stop it at dead-centre or "straight arm" may have contributed. "May" is said advisedly for the inconvenience can easily be exaggerated and probably never really bothered a practised driver any more than it troubled the driver of a single cylinder threshing engine.

The work of showmen's engines initially was limited to haulage and generating for electric light or organs. Bioscope shows requiring electricity appeared about 1900 (though gas-lit

The typical showman's road train! Smith & Warren of Lincoln ready for the road. The engine is possibly the Burrell 8nhp single-crank compound No 1985 Mona I

shows came four or five years earlier) and scenic railways about 1910. The problems of load associated with the starting up led to the scenic type showman's engine with both a dynamo and an exciter based on Hackett and Whatman's patent of 1911. A scenic railway knocked down made nine loads—about the capacity of the engine for road haulage.

Circuses and menageries took less readily than riding machine proprietors to the steam engine for haulage—probably because they feared the effect the steam engines might have of making their livestock uneasy. Bostock and Wombwell had the famous 5hp Burrells *Rajah* and *Nero* together with a Robey tractor and, briefly, a Burrell 4hp tractor, but nevertheless relied heavily on draught horses until the surplus Army vehicles of World War I made internal combustion engine lorries an economic proposition. Many beast shows indeed went straight from horses to the motor, though on the other hand "The Great Carmo" (née Stott) had most of his circus steam-hauled in the nineteen-twenties, albeit mainly with steam wagons. Steam lasted until the final disastrous

A view of the opposite side of the engine, showing it set up on the fairground for generating. Single-crank compounds like this one gave way to double-crank compounds in the esteem of showmen in the early years of the century

fire at Blackpool in 1929 which put an end to the show.

Travelling a ride was always an occupation that demanded a lot of effort for a relatively small return, particularly with horses. Not long before he died, Billy Nunn of Hunstanton described to the writer how his father used to travel a small pony-powered roundabout through the Norfolk villages with his young sons. Mrs Nunn had no taste for travelling and stayed at home where she kept a small street-corner shop. Billy related that his father, after a season's hard work came home delighted.

"We've had a good summer, Mother—eight pounds ten clear".

Admittedly out of this they had eaten well, had taken a little ale and had fed the horses but even so, it was not much as the net gain of a whole summer.

Competition was keen also. Although each firm had a "permanent address" this had little bearing upon the roads they covered and shows ranged the length and breadth of the county constantly trying to be first of the season on a pitch, always endeavouring to steal a march on one another, always at rivalry at a big fair as to who could build-up or pull-down fastest. Shows would be pulled down after the fair closed late at night, travelled to the next pitch and built-up for an opening the following evening. It is said that Gray's moved from Hampstead to Kings Lynn with a scenic

Bert Stock's ex-WD Garrett 4nhp tractor photographed near Ipswich. The first load is the centre truck of the ride still on wooden wheels with iron bushes, the cause of so many headaches to showmen's drivers

[R. G. Pratt

Burrell double-crank compound No 3302 John Bull *new in July 1911 to Barker & Thurston of Norwich, photographed in Christchurch Park, Ipswich*

[R. G. Pratt]

Burrell and loads in a single autumn day— but what a day!

This rivalry led the major showmen into constant competition for new and novel rides— the circular railway, the Razzle Dazzle, the steam yachts, the scenic railway—and, in a slightly different field, into the bioscope shows. From these came the static cinema, the biggest single blow the fairground ever received. Some mastermen left off travelling and became proprietors of cinemas but others thought it just another novelty that would pass and went off after other things. Mrs Dougal Reynolds (Vi Forrest) summed this up nicely when she said, "My dad had a bioscope show in the Mile End Road next to one that Sidney Bernstein's father ran and he gave it up because he thought there was no future in it. Now look what Sidney Bernstein's got and what we've got!" It should perhaps be added that though the millions had evaded the Forrests they were nevertheless living comfortably and prosperously and enjoying the satisfaction and independence of travelling their own show.

By the nineteen-twenties intense competition both between individual showmen and with the cinema was eating away profits. The formation of the Showmen's Guild, nominally for the protection of showmen, was in fact destined to protect them as much from themselves as from outside enemies by promoting agreements on the territories to be travelled and consequently reducing the annual wasted mileage. This notwithstanding, shows still travelled and in the not over adventurous village life the author led as a boy it was always an event when the showmen's road train appeared down the hill into the village, with men running beside the loads working the brakes and the engine probably stopping to sneak a drink out of the horse-trough.

CHAPTER 3

The Engineman

"Some kids are brought up on skim milk;
And some are brought up on cream,
And some are brought up on nothing;
But I was brought up on steam".
The Passing of the Steam Locomotive.
J. Collopy.

IT IS all too easy and attractive, as traction engines at work recede into history, to exalt the men who worked with them into a gallery of heroes, larger and nobler than life. It is a fact nevertheless that the impact of the traction engine upon the rural community did draw out a group of men as noted in their way for their strength of character and tenacity as were the railway enginemen whose emergence had come a generation before.

The agricultural traction engine first became numerically significant about the year 1870, as noted in Chapter 1. English agriculture was at that time nearing the end of one of its cyclic periods of high prosperity but little of the effects of the prosperity had rubbed off on to the farm worker. There was a division among the employed between those on a weekly footing—the horsemen, cowmen, stockmen and shepherds—and the day men who were paid on a daily basis and who, on wet days or other occasions when work was impossible, were sent home unpaid. The wage of a farm labourer in regular work were of the order of ten shillings a week with a few privileges in the way perhaps of cheap milk and free firewood. The weekly men were somewhat better off. They lived in the cottages on the farm itself, usually superior to the labourer's cottages in the village, enjoyed cheap milk supplies and

firewood, had ground upon which they could grow vegetables, keep a few chickens and rabbits or perhaps a pig and often allowances of wheat and barley, from which latter it was common practice to brew beer at home. In cash, however, their incomes were still small ranging from 11 shillings to 12s as a shepherd to perhaps 17s or 18s as a head horseman on a large farm. The actual rates varied a little from area to area and even from farm to farm but the relationships remained much the same.

The steps in the wage ladder were matched by an established pecking order in the personal plane. The day men were regarded as much lower than the weekly men but again the latter were rigidly divided into a hierarchy of their own and nowhere less than in the stable. Turning-out was a carefully observed ritual— the head horseman first, then the head horse-man's mate followed by the second horseman and his mate. A departure from this order of precedence meant a sharp reprimand or a rebuke in kind.

The head horseman, indeed, was an important stone in the intricate social structure of a large farm. Frequently he was selected to be "Lord of the Harvest", a title of which the origin was lost in history or possibly even pre-history, responsible for the oversight of the cutting in the harvest field, the carting and the building of the corn stacks, especially the outsides and corners for the corn might stand in the stack well into the winter before being threshed.

The carefully regulated positions of the men on the farm relative to one another, the survival of superstitions and practices from the middle ages, the poor chances of escape from the system, except by emigration to the industrial towns or overseas, and the humble circumstances of even the top men cannot have failed to chafe on capable and energetic young men. Enlistment in the army or navy provided one escape route, service in a great house another, but the eruption of the steam engine on to the rural scene provided a diversion of a totally different sort, an incursion of progress and modernity into the apparently timeless rural scene.

This timelessness was not so real as it appeared for the working of the land in large farms did not in fact go back much beyond the middle of the eighteenth century before which the common field and the manorial waste had been the dominant features of agriculture. The odd intermingling of one farm with another which is still evident in modern holdings, derives often from the break-up of the system. By the mid eighteen-sixties, however, farming and the state of the farm worker had been what they were for long enough to seem immemorial.

Whenever a traction engine and portable threshing machine was first put to work in a district there was, as a rule, no local man available with steam experience to man it. The driver would, therefore, be either an outsider, trained and provided by the makers or a local man selected by the owner to be instructed in its use either by being sent to the maker's works or by a driver-instructor sent with the set or both. An incoming driver from one of the industrial towns would have no reverence whatever for such shibboleths as the carefully nurtured status of the head horseman and stockman. Secure in the knowledge that none of them could assail his own knowledge or competence he was entirely free to debunk

their pretensions and to make light of the jealousies of a small closed community and since he was seldom on one farm for more than a few days at a time they had little opportunity to get back at him. Sometimes a man like this stayed many years with his first rural employer but others moved on after a short time leaving the local man who had been the steersman to carry on as a driver. Even if the "foreign" driver stayed, the acquisition of a second engine and drum more or less automatically promoted his steersman to driver.

However recruited, the threshing driver was an individual quite outside what was regarded as the natural order of things, with no roots into the practices of the past, experience not only of his own but of a dozen neighbouring villages and, it was often suspected, a marked disrespect for the law and for the disciplines of the farm.

This suspicion was undoubtedly well founded. It is impossible to be long in the company of a group of engine drivers without the conversation getting round to the artful dodges and deceptions practised upon the village constable and others in authority. To the constable, the thresher crew were "travelling men" and therefore liable to be lumped with gypsies, tinkers, travelling showmen, actors and other itinerants under a common cloud of suspicion. The troubles engines and their drivers had with the law are treated in the next chapter and it is sufficient to say here that relations between drivers and the police were seldom cordial. Steam threshing, however, though it may have upset the old rules, imposed disciplines of its own.

The timetable of a threshing driver would run something like this. Rise at 4 30am, wash (usually with cold water), drink a cup of tea and leave home around 5 0am for a walk of up to an hour's duration to reach the engine. Sweep the tubes and smokebox and light up the engine, start threshing at 7 0am. Stop about 9 0am for breakfast, continue until midday when a break of half an hour (sometimes an hour) was taken, finish threshing about 5 0pm. After this the engine had to be clinkered out, the ashpan emptied, the wicks lifted out of the oil feed tubes and the engine sheeted up. Leave the engine about 5 45pm and arrive home about 6 45pm. This sort of timetable was kept by the driver in all sorts of winter weather and some-times up to an advanced age. The job was not always ten miles from home and the weather was not invariably freezing but even with the most mitigating circumstances it was a de-manding occupation.

In the earliest days of threshing by steam hauled tackle, the house-van seems not to have been used and the men either walked to and from home, if at all possible, daily, or failing that, slept rough in a barn or shed or even under the engine. Later the old sit up and beg bicycle became a great standby and drivers would cycle quite long distances—ten miles was by no means uncommon—to work, but by then the house van had come into use for the more distant work. Living vans were first used with steam ploughing tackle and few references are found to their being used with threshers before the 'eighties.

Living in the van was a somewhat mixed blessing. It enabled the threshing crew to be early on the job without the journey to work but it also posed the problem of housekeeping, cooking and general personal cleanliness. Some drivers went to great pains to keep themselves and their vans just so and spent a great deal of the spare time cleaning either the van or the

Engineman absent! Ruston & Proctor No 36828 6nhp single-cylinder traction engine owned by Percy Kingsnorth and his late father at Great Chart near Ashford, Kent

E

engine. A driver, now dead, employed by a Wealden firm (we will call him Jack) was not so fussy. When living on the job in a van he never reckoned to undress at night. A mate who was sent with him to a contract on Romney Marsh complained on his return after having had to share a bunk with him, "I didn't mind the old b—— getting into bed in his overalls but he might ha' taken his boots off."

Yet another misadventure in house van living that comes to mind concerns the late Amos "Shucks" Arnold who drove for James Penfold Ltd of Arundel. Like many others, Amos liked a few pints in the evening. As a consequence of this hobby he returned to the van one dark night, half seas over and hungry. Fumbling in the food cupboard by candlelight he found a few cold potatoes and some bacon and had a fry-up. Next morning his mate asked him, "What did you do last night, Shucks?"

"Oh, I had a bit of a fry-up, a few potatoes and a bit of bacon I found in the cupboard."

"What'd you cook it in?"

"Oh, a bit of fat I found in a tin."

"You dizzy old fool, there weren't no fat. That was black oil you fried 'em in."

Shucks seldom lacked eggs when his van was on a farm. He explained that he never closed the van door whilst he was at work and always contrived to leave a little grain scattered on its steps and floor from the handful or two he kept in his pocket. Could he be held to blame if a hen found his old coat a convenient nesting place?

Lonely evenings in a living van drove many a man to the delights of the local alehouse though with pubs open all day it was not only in the evenings that drivers drank. Beer or cider was at the root of a great many of the troubles that overtook engines and it was not so much actual drunkenness as loss of time that often produced trouble. Engines over driven to make up time thus lost and tampering with safety valves to give the engine the necessary extra urge were the two commonest mischiefs that followed too long a stop at the public house.

The wages of an engine-driver as the nineteenth century entered its last quarter were the order of twenty shillings a week—ten per cent more than the wages of the highest grade of farm worker—with the opportunity to earn tips from the more liberal farmers. With good beer at a penny a pint the thresher driver could afford, like the steam ploughman, to thump on the counter and shout his orders. In 1879, however, the agricultural community, already being pressed by the newly developed cornfields of Australia and North America, suffered the final disaster of the worst summer for perhaps two hundred years. Crops over huge areas were lost and even where brought to harvest yielded poor crops of inferior grain. Two more indifferent summers followed and by the early 'eighties agriculture was in an abyss from which it began to recover only by the mid-nineties.

During this depression few new threshing sets were put to work and the race of engine drivers was not much enlarged. With the revival, however, new engines and threshers were bought as confidence returned and most of the mechanical oddities that had survived through the hungry years were replaced by modern engines. The influx of new drivers provided the basis of the corps who manned engines until the end of their commercial use and of the rich vein of individualism that permeated it.

Arthur Jenner, who for many years drove a set for Walter Arnold & Sons of Paddock Wood, Kent, was noted for his punctuality. He would regularly arrive at the engine well before six o'clock in the morning, after cycling several miles, and usually much earlier on a Monday when he had to raise steam from dead cold. Arthur, like many other set foremen, was of a somewhat cantankerous disposition. It was unwise, indeed, to attempt to converse with him before ten in the morning and his comments up to that time were customarily confined to castigating the rest of the threshing gang.

The only compensation enjoyed by the latter was that they could answer him any way they wished behind his back for he was stone deaf and could converse only by lip reading. This deafness was his undoing on at least one occasion. The old man had moved the drum into the stackyard at Little Trench Farm, Tonbridge, now built over, using the pole, had carefully levelled the thresher with the jacks, set up the ladder and made ready for work. Satisfied with what he had done he quickly climbed up on the manstand, for despite his years he was pretty agile, and drew the engine forward preparatory to running round the drum to set it for work. Sad to relate he had forgotten the pole. The drum snatched forward, upsetting the chocks and throwing over the ladder, a new one just issued to him. All the gang bellowed a warning but he did not hear a word and in fact noticed what was happening only when he felt the load on the engine. By this time the drum wheel had run over the ladder and all was confusion. The old man was furious. "Why didn't someone shout", he stormed.

Both he and Stan Jacques, a Durham man who drove for the same firm, sometimes managed to do three "half days" daily. Because both were quick on the road and fast at setting up the drum they were at times able to fit three small threshing jobs into one day. As the firm never invoiced less than a half day's hire they thus got three of them into one working day.

As remarked earlier the engine driver's great standby for personal transport was the old high safety bicycle, the driver's bike, hung up on the rear of the thresher, being a recognised part of the equipment of a threshing set on the move. In the period between the wars some of the more adventurous or better-off members of the fraternity used motor cycles but the old push-bike remained the norm giving way occasionally to the tricycle. A well-known trike rider in the West Kent area of the writer's youth was 'Uncle' Leigh who drove Fowler single No 9832 for the firm of Day & Hale of

A group of enginemen taken in 1908. The man on the left is Edmund Pack, a well-known driver in Kent and Sussex, employed by Charles Hooker of Egerton. Walter Hooker, son of Pack's employer is the moustached man on the right. The name of the mate in the middle is not recorded. The dress is typical of enginemen at that period

[C. E. Hooker

Penshurst. Like Arthur Jenner he was noted for his irascible temper though unlike Walter's his hearing was normal and he was able to catch the retorts of his mate, his son Lew, who as an ex-sailor was seldom lost for words. The sight of the whiskery old man crouched over the boiler front, his face flecked with black oil spots thrown off the crankshaft of the four shaft engine, usually in a most disreputable old cap with an unbuttoned peak and usually in a hurry —for he was not averse to a jar or two in the pub—was a thing not readily forgotten. For years he and Lew had an extra shilling from their employers for washing out on Sundays. Then things changed, for it was about the time of the slump, and the edict went out that as washing out was inseparable from the job there was no justification for the extra shilling and it was to cease. "Right", said Uncle' "so does the Sunday morning," and thereafter he washed out on Saturday morning, costing the firm at least a couple of hours work with the thresher which has always seemed to the writer a good example of an Irish economy. Uncle was a most excellent driver, not only on the road but also at getting into and out of awkward yards and in looking after the engine which he and Lew kept in repair. Between them they put in new tubes, renewed stays and on one occasion put a screwed and stayed patch on to the fire side, cutting out the distressed plate by means of overlapping holes drilled with a ratchet brace and the old flat drills, which they kept trooping across to Tommy Skinner's forge opposite to sharpen. That and a few trips to the Wheatsheaf was all that broke the monotony of about three days drilling and this, not in a shed or workshop, but in the corner of a field.

Whilst it is difficult to remember Uncle other than as a likeable old reprobate it is not fair to conclude a glance at the threshing driver without a look at the other face of the medal. By the last quarter of the century the evangelical movement in the Church of England, the upsurge of the free churches and the emergence of the Salvation Army had produced a large scale reaction against heavy drinking or indeed the taking of alcohol in any quantities and though the engine driving fraternity on the whole never forsook its partiality for ale, an appreciable minority defected to the ranks of teetotalism. To poke fun at this group was easy—perhaps it still is—but nevertheless they provided a valuable curb or counter balance to the drinking sector of their craft. In their lifetimes many of them must have despaired of influencing their fellows but in retrospect they can be seen to have had their effect. The late Baden Parsons of St Columb, Cornwall,

was a notable and affectionately remembered example of the militantly teetotal engine-driver. Fervently religious, he was never deflected from his belief even by grievous disappointments in his life, notably when, because of his father's omission to make a will, he failed to inherit a share of the threshing business he had laboured long and unrewarded to establish. Not long before he died he related how, caught by a torrential thunderstorm one Saturday night on the engine—which like many Cornish engines fortunately had a roof—he and his mate sang Sankey and Moody hymns whilst the lightning flashed and the thunder shook.

Nevertheless it is the stories of devilment and oddity that make the best telling, such as that of the 'Mad' Davis's, noted for their wild antics and hilarious goings on. Always working at a frantic rate they were threshing with their Clayton traction and drum in a tight stackyard on the border of Herefordshire and Wales, using a gutta-percha belt. Two sheaves landed on the apron together and by inadvertence or carelessness the feeder let both go into the drum together where they jammed up. The governors opened the valve wide under the load, the engine, which as usual was right up to pressure, gave a series of barks like cannon shots, the gutta-percha belt refused to slip and before anyone could lift a hand to stop the mischief the drum was wound smartly up to the engine smokebox which it hit with a crash at last throwing off the belt but not before staving in the end of the drum.

Also from the Welsh border is the story of the Fowler engine which with the drum, trusser and elevator was driven by the deaf and dumb son of its owner. As the driver and his mate, Charlie Edwards, were finishing off their day's work, the owner arrived in his dog cart. It was already late and dusk was not far off, for the last of the threshing had taken longer than expected but nevertheless the father insisted that his son should move on to the next farm that night so as not to interfere with the next day's work. Consequently they set off against the judgement of the crew into the rapidly gathering dusk. Before long they were running by lamp light down a very narrow but fairly straight lane. Disaster was near, however, for at the end of the straight the lane took a left turn leaving a duck pond straight ahead. Put off their bearings by the dark, driver and mate missed the turn and before either could do anything the engine was in the pond. Though not badly in, they could do nothing to extricate themselves because of the loads behind. The owner was shouting and cursing, the engine, being nose down, began to blow-off, and the crew faced getting down into the stinking water to get ashore. Charlie was sent on across several fields to knock up the farmer's horsemen to bring out their horses, which, of course, had been stabled for the night, to pull back the loads after which they roped themselves clear and finished the last quarter mile or so of the journey. "We used to pride ourselves on keeping her a bit decent like," recalled Charles, "but man, you should have seen her."

Engine drivers were not popular lodgers. Even those who washed carefully were usually unable to remove the last residue of black from their hands, faces and hair, whilst coal dust in the boots did nothing for the state of their feet and the careful washers were by no means a majority. This residual dirt left its mark upon the bed clothes which tended to discourage the admission of drivers to the better type of lodgings and to force them into accommodation run by those who had less heed for cleanliness. This caught the long distance drivers with particular force and many, especially those on furniture bumping where long hauls were the rule, took to sleeping with the load whenever the state of the weather or the nature of the load did not prohibit it. With a furniture moving team of four, two of the crew had anyway to ride with the load and usually managed to arrange the contents of the vans so that a comfortable corner was provided. This refuge doubled up at night as a sleeping place. Not only did sleeping in this way save the expense

of dubious lodgings but it helped to ensure that no one tampered with engine or loads at night.

Arthur Pipe, of the Garrett concern, relates how he once helped the purchaser of a new engine (a steam wagon) to drive it home to Manchester. By leaving Leiston soon after dawn and driving by turns they reached Manchester the same night between 11 opm and midnight—a considerable feat in itself. Arthur was taken to the house of his companion's brother where he was to sleep. After much thumping on the door the brother came downstairs in his overalls, in which he had apparently been sleeping, followed by his wife in a man's overcoat over a nightdress. Mugs of tea were brewed up and they sat round the table at midnight by gaslight, each with a mug of tea and, in the centre of the table, a tin of Nestle's milk and one spoon which they used in turn to add the thick sweet milk to the contents of their respective cups. Arthur was then shown by candle up to bed, which he was to share with a young man who was to set out about four the next morning with the brother who was acting as host. He, too, proved to be partly clothed as he rolled out of bed without too much complaint, to let Arthur have the place next to the wall. Four hours later he got up, waking Arthur who lay awake as the daylight gradually dawned, revealing that the bed-clothes were practically black. Though a tolerant man he came from a home where the standards of house-keeping were impeccable. "Believe me," he said, "I was up and out of that house before five, notwithstanding the hours we had spent on the road the day before."

There were, of course, drivers who solved the sleeping problem neither by the lodging house nor by dossing in a house van or amongst their load but simply by sleeping under the engine. Such a one was the redoubtable 'Pincher' who drove a Clayton road engine for Charles Miles, the sawmiller of Stamford, Lincolnshire. Whatever the season Pincher slept wrapped in a tarpaulin beneath the boiler and if his pet sometimes dripped black oil upon him he seemed not to mind. Pincher liked working in the open and in remote places which was just as well for with the enormous quantities of beer he consumed he had somewhat eccentric personal habits. Pincher was a very rough and rather grubby old man but the fact remains that when he gave up work the Clayton had to be laid off too for there was simply not another like him.

Round timber haulage was one of the most consistently hard occupations for steam haulage and it is not surprising, therefore, that it harboured a high proportion of men like Pincher, incredibly hardy and dextrous despite a rough hewn exterior. The extraction of big round timber from the wood, except during the few dry months of the English summer, involving wire-roping forwards, perhaps of both the engine and the load, was a matter of sheer slog. Loading it involved a higher skill—a skill in fact disputed as between driver and loader. Though the driver required a nice finesse in handling the reversing lever and the throttle it was the loader who had to decide how to place the tree trunk in relation to the tug and the skids and where to position the rope and chains for rolling it up. Error in any of these points made loading impossible since unless the rope was at the point of balance the log would cant to one end or the other whilst wrong positioning of the tree in relation to the tug, if it did not upset the placing of the rope at point of balance, would have meant that the log, if loaded, would not sit well on the carriage. It was the loader's lot also to ride with the load, manipulate the brakes, open and close gates, flag down other road traffic and generally carry out the chores of the outfit. In most outfits living on the job, whether in a van or in the open, he was also the cook.

Strange things sometimes found their way into the cooking. Wild birds' eggs in season, rook, hedgehog, moorhen, pigeon and rabbit all openly found their way on to the menu— pheasant, partridge, grouse and woodcock surreptitiously—with the engine firebox always a

handy way of disposing of feet, heads and feathers. Living thus off the land left more money for necessities. Many years ago Rookery Wood at Leigh, near Tonbridge, was cleared by a gang of such timber fellers and hauliers who did for themselves, mainly by sleeping in the straw in the barns of Ramhurst Manor nearby. Each evening they were to be found in the Plough Inn supping beer or cider and smoking large pipefuls of a rough shag. One evening when the weather was bitter an old man of the gang sat there by the fire with the toe of his boot gaping from the sole. It was too much for one of the locals. "I should've thought you'd ha' got some new boots before buying so much beer", he observed. The grey beard contemplated his battered footwear with equanimity. Quite without heat he replied, "Ah—beer an' baccy we must have—boots we can do without".

Akin to the timber hauliers were the steam sawyers. Though it was not feasible to set up a full scale sawmill so to speak "on location" the portable rack bench was a very handy tool for converting tops and lower grade timber into gate posts, rails and gate material and many a farm or estate that did not rate an estate sawmill was able at intervals to use the travelling saw, the arrival of which was a village event in a round of life not noted for excitement. The plentiful supply of chips and small off-cuts attracted the thrifty village women in search of firing and as the sawyers were there during the day when the village men were not, it is said that a good looking sawyer could find himself in possession of a kind of *droit de seigneur* with the warmer maidens and matrons even to the point it is alleged of facilitating the transition of the former to the latter. Whether commerce by barter was carried to these lengths or not it certainly procured for the sawyers many of the lesser necessities of life— potatoes, cabbage, eggs and onions though not often meat or cheese.

Barter was a chronic disease amongst steam roller drivers too. Sidney Buncombe, son of

An unusual engine photographed outside its proper habitat. A Ransomes, Sims & Jefferies single-cylinder Colonial type pictured whilst in use by the makers as a works engine at Ipswich. The very long chimney does nothing for its appearance

[R. G. Pratt collection

the late principal of the roller owning firm of W. W. Buncombe & Sons Ltd of Highbridge, Somerset, related not long since how, years ago, he arrived in Wantage to visit one of their rollers which had been on hire for a long while at the nearby village of ——. Pausing for lunch at the Bear Hotel he asked the waitress if she could tell him the way to ——.

"Oh yes sir," she replied, "I live there."

"Well you probably know my steam roller that is working there then", said Sidney.

"Yes, I do", answered the girl, "And a very nice man drives it. He puts a bag of coal on our wall and my mother puts up cabbages".

By way of an aside and as an illustration of the low returns from roller ownership about 1930 it may be related how Sid Buncombe's father, the late W. W. 'Billy' Buncombe, remarked at one of the earliest meetings of the Road Roller Owners' Association, "Well, I've got two hundred rollers and if each one earns me no more than five shillings a week that's fifty pounds".

The seasonal nature of both road rolling and threshing was a bugbear to owners and drivers alike. Before about 1910 roads were mainly waterbound and were repaired in the autumn and winter months from October to March leaving the balance of the year when rollers were mainly unemployed. To meet this objection the roller convertible to a traction engine was evolved. Other firms owned both tractions and rollers but either way there was always an annual period of unemployment for some drivers. From 1910 onwards the proportion of tarred and tarmacadamed roads increased annually giving for a time full roller employment but finally, with the disappearance of waterbound macadam, the cycle was reversed with full roller usage during the warm months and very much reduced demand during the rest of the year. In these years, say 1919-1939, owners often had both rollers and threshing sets to give a reasonably continuous income but the overlapping did not wholly permeate the trade and there was always a winter period when some rollermen were out of work.

In the heavy haulage field there was a sharp cleavage into the showmen and "the rest". Showmen's work, except for the fortunate few who had lucrative winter pitches, was strictly seasonal the extremes being Easter and Michaelmas. Drivers and steersmen, if not members of the owner's family, were engaged for the season and as the word got round, either by word of mouth or by an advertisement, that old "so and so" wanted a driver, hopeful applicants would appear at his winter quarters. Some owners took on the same driver year after year but others never seemed to have the same man twice. Beach's *Bertha* is an engine that seems to have been driven at some time by just about every driver in the business. Allowing for a proportion of false claims or bad memories the turnover could fairly be described as considerable. Some showmen's drivers, like the late and ever to be lamented Tom Glover, were men of the greatest skill and highest integrity—of others the least said the better. It was once remarked to the writer, "When the travellers came into the bar the publican even took the cat off the counter." To be fair, however, the fairground owed its spicy reputation more to the "gaff lads"—the seasonal hands—than to the drivers and the mates, curious characters though some of the latter were.

So far as "the rest" of the heavy haulage scene was concerned the work was in the hands of a limited number of highly specialised firms such as Pickfords, Coulsons of Park Royal, Norman Box of Manchester, Coupe Brothers of Sheffield, Kerr of Mavisbank, E. W. Rudd of London, Robert Wynn of Cardiff and John Harkness of Belfast, to mention the names of a few of the select band. Long distance steam haulage never really bloomed until this century and was at its zenith in the 1920s. Ships and power stations provided many of the outstanding loads moved by engines closely followed by transformer equipment, the paraphernalia of oil refineries and heavy equipment for steel works and forges. The actual list of heavy articles transported is too extensive to stand repetition but it was a traffic that went on throughout the year and hard slog though it was the men who followed it had a more or less constant livelihood, whether they were Rudd's irrepressible Cockneys, Coupe's Yorkshiremen or Kerr's Glaswegians. To meet such a load on the road—a hundred-ton transformer perhaps—with three engines hauling and a steam tractor following up with the living van and coal, was a sight not readily to be forgotten. The pace was slow, every awkward corner or cross-roads an adventure and there seemed always to be men running alongside. In the afternoon one might find the crew resting and the load pulled off the road outside a big town so that it could pass through in the quiet hours from midnight to six o'clock. One night the writer was sleeping at the Crown at Oakham, Rutland, when there were obviously unusual and exciting sounds from the street below which, on investigation, proved to be Rudds with an enormous sheeted object on a well wagon, complete with police escort and outriders. After a few minutes the foreman got into the police car and went off, presumably to prospect the road ahead.

"Where's old Blank?" called a driver, clearly with reference to the foreman. "Gorn orf in the police car", was the answer; then wistfully came the reply, "Blimey I 'ope they keep 'im".

The policemen in this case seemed to be

The skill of the heavy haulage crew. Back view of the loading of a rotor at Manchester. The trolley is typical of the crude but sturdy vehicles used for short distances
[Entwistle and Thorpe

The other side of the task. The work was done by only six men and two engines without any plant beyond the engines and trolley and timber packing
[Entwistle and Thorpe

enjoying themselves and to be getting some amusement out of the haulage crew, rather in contrast to the attitude of earlier generations of police who appeared, at any rate in the eyes of the enginemen, to take a delight in persecuting engines, their owners and their drivers.

Emitting smoke, blowing off steam on the highway, and failure to display a spark arrester, all attracted the unwelcome attention of the law. The stock answer, propounded by Frank Penfold of Arundel, Sussex, to the policeman getting too pointed in his questions about the spark arrester was, "It's fitted inside and if you don't believe me climb up and have a look". Few did.

The works staff of Thomas Wood and Son, Crockenhill, Kent, in about 1911

[Thomas Wood & Son

CHAPTER 4

Engines in Trouble

"Misfortune has come upon us all together,
The poor, the rich, the weak and the strong".

An Irish poem,
translated by Lady Gregory

THE TRACTION ENGINE was subjected, during its lifetime, to more than its fair share of legal harassments. The causes to which this is commonly attributed are ignorance and prejudice and although there was probably no shortage of either a hundred and forty years ago, it is wrong to suppose that the outlook of the mass of the population influenced either the structure or the actions of the legislature.

The legislature in fact took no repressive action during what may be termed the "steam carriage" period of development and it was not until the Locomotive Act of 1861 that Parliament intervened in the regulation of self-propelled road vehicles.

In 1831 when the claims of steam carriages were being strenuously canvassed the lower house appointed a select committee to study the subject, after prodding by Goldsworthy Gurney's complaint against excessive turnpike tolls. The committee's report stated, *inter alia*:

"1 That carriages can be propelled by steam on common roads at an average rate of ten miles per hour;

2 That at this rate they have conveyed upwards of fourteen passengers;

3 That their weight, including engine, fuel, water and attendants may be under three tons;

4 That they can ascend and descend hills of considerable inclination with facility and safety;

5 That they are perfectly safe for passengers;

6 That they are not (or need not be if properly constructed) nuisances to the public;

7 That they will become a speedier and cheaper mode of conveyance than carriages drawn by horses;

8 That as they admit of greater breadth of tire than other carriages and as the roads are not acted on so injuriously as by the feet of horses in common draught, such carriages will cause less wear of roads than coaches drawn by horses;

9 That rates of toll have been imposed on steam carriages which would prohibit their being used on several lines of road, were such charges permitted to remain unaltered".

Notwithstanding the committee's favourable report no legislative changes were made in favour of steam carriages, probably because of Parliament's preoccupation with the Russell reforms, notably and pre-eminently the Reform Act of 1832, nor did the convening of two further committees in 1832 and 1835, to report upon Gurney's claim for an extension of his patent and his claim for pecuniary compensation in respect of the loss he alleged he had sustained as a result of legislation unfavourable to his steam carriages, have any more beneficial effect.

Parliament underwent a radical change between 1831 and 1834 as a result of the Reform Act of 1832 which not only rearranged constituencies and redistributed seats but enfranchised large numbers of the well-to-do middle class who had not before had an influential part in Parliamentary elections. In the interval, Turnpike Acts had continued to be passed with little discussion or opposition and it was through these that the steam vehicle sustained its legislative setbacks, mainly in the shape of penal tolls. Turnpiking was a method of securing the construction, alteration or repair of roads by the creation of trusts empowered to execute the necessary work and to recoup their expenses by levelling tolls. Trustees were drawn from local property owners and from the justices of the peace of the county or counties in which the road forming the subject of the trust was situated. The general legislation creating turnpike trusts was contained in a group of Acts known as the General Turnpike Acts. Individual trusts were created by specific Acts known as Local Acts which nominated the persons to act as trustees and the toll to be levied. Though the method of levying tolls on horse traffic was stated, few acts contemplated mechanical transport and consequently the trustees, when they wished, were able to levy extortionate tolls upon steam carriages. These excessive charges were, however, carried through into fresh trusts enacted after the appearance of steam carriages and it must be concluded, therefore, that, notwithstanding the favourable report of the 1831 select committee, Parliament was prepared to turn a blind eye to the levying of tolls specifically designed to repress the steam carriage.

It would thus seem a fair assumption that the class of persons from which turnpike trustees were drawn constituted the main source of opposition to steam on roads—that is to say what the contemporary countryman would have called "the gentry", a generic term covering all landowners from the minor squirearchy to the most noble patricians. The reasons for the opposition are less clear. Possibly the steam carriages were felt to be yet another aspect of the hateful wave of change following the Napoleonic Wars that was encroaching upon their position or it may have been that a more direct influence was the fear, only too well justified, that the rise of road motors would be a crushing blow to the fodder and bedding trade which was such a prop to the rural economy. Certainly it is clear that the source of opposition was not a railway lobby for the mileage of railway at the time was trivial. This opposition by the landowners of the country is confirmed by the fate of a Bill introduced into Parliament in 1836 aimed at relieving steam carriages from exorbitant tolls. The Bill passed the reformed Commons but failed in the Lords, the stronghold of the landed gentry.

Had the railways not spread across the country so rapidly it is doubtful if the opposition to the steam road vehicle could have held it at bay for so long in the face of the demands of the country's economy for faster and more effective land transport. As it was, the opposition had the effect of driving traffic into the arms of the railway companies and of dampening down interest in the steam carriages to negligible proportions.

By the time, however, when the traction engine was beginning to be an effective force— the early eighteen-sixties—the sources of opposition had altered though the franchise had not. Turnpike trusts, where not already defunct, were moribund but in consequence of the discouragement of road transport thirty years earlier, there was an immense railway lobby not only because of direct financial interest but because of the genuinely held belief that it was in the national interest to foster rail traffic at the expense of roads. The railway company provided its own right of way and everything necessary to regulate and maintain its traffic, even to its own police force.

On the contrary every extension of traffic on the roads led firstly to extra maintenance and secondly to a demand for improvements, the costs of both of which fell upon the localities in which the road happened to be situated and not upon the places in which the traffic originated. Thus London to Birmingham road traffic would have brought a burden of road costs to towns and parishes not participating in the slightest in the benefits the traffic bestowed. Many completely disinterested Members of Parliament undoubtedly honestly held the view that to take any steps that would divert traffic from rail to road were bound to result in higher local taxation.

The Locomotive Act 1861 (24 and 25 Vict. Cap. 70) was the child of the declining years of Palmerston's last ministry in which Gladstone was Chancellor of the Exchequer and, since many of the Act's provisions were fiscal, probably its sponsor. So upright a minister is unlikely to have embarked upon an Act whose intention was oppressive and indeed the preface and first five sections of the Act which relieved locomotives and their loads of oppressive tolls and regulated the construction and weight of vehicles were sound. Section 6, however, gave highway surveyors or others responsible for bridges the right to bar engines from bridges that, in their opinion, were insufficiently strong to sustain the weight, a provision outwardly reasonable and sensible that became a cruelly restrictive device in the hand of biased local authorities. The following section contained the infamous provision that damage caused by locomotives to bridges was repairable at the expense of the engine owner, without placing any similar burden upon the owners of horsedrawn vehicles, whilst section 8 required a locomotive to consume its own smoke.

This section and the one following, which regulated the number of men who were to attend a road train, were repealed in the Locomotive Act, 1865, more explicit clauses covering smoke and steam emission being substituted

and the notorious "red flag" provision being enacted under which the flag man had to carry his flag sixty yards ahead of the locomotive to warn horse traffic and provide assistance to it in passing the engine. Specifically drivers were prohibited from allowing safety valves to blow off on the road. Engines were limited to a width of nine feet and fourteen tons in weight both of which were reasonable limitations in their time.

Again reasonably the Act repealed insofar as ploughing engines were concerned, section 70 of the Highway Act 1835 which prohibited the erection and working of a steam engine within twenty-five yards of a highway, a provision which had been construed as prohibiting the use of ploughing engines within that distance. The owner's name and address had to be displayed on the engine and speeds were restricted to two miles per hour in cities, towns and villages and four miles per hour elsewhere.

Possibly its worst provision was that which authorised local authorities to declare prohibited hours during which locomotives could not be worked upon the roads under their jurisdiction without limiting the hours during which such working might be prohibited, a most inequitable power which was shamefully abused. Subsequently it was curtailed by the Highways and Locomotives (Amendment) Act of 1878 which restricted prohibited hours to eight out of any twenty-four—still giving authorities scope for plenty of mischief.

The 1865 Act was the high point of the tide of repression—thereafter legislation became gradually less punitive and though the Act of 1878 was a mild affair it mitigated the worst aspect of the law as it stood by abolishing the red flag and allowing the look-out man to be only twenty yards ahead, by introducing the words "so far as practicable" into the clause requiring self-consumption of smoke and by authorising the use of cross strakes on wheels, removing an ambiguity of the 1861 Act which had been construed (Stringer v. Sykes in the Exchequer Division of the High Court) as requiring strakes to be nine inches wide. The wording of the 1861 Act, "with shoes or other bearing surface of a width not less than nine inches", was probably meant to cover the Boydell engine and the subsequent distortion of its meaning is a good example of the kind of manoeuvres of the anti-engine faction.

Another example is Body v. Jeffrey. Here the wheels were eighteen inches wide, shod with shoes nine and three quarter inches wide, three inches broad and one inch thick laid alternately round the wheel, their inner edges touching for about an inch and a quarter so that there was always a bearing surface of at least nine inches in one continuous width on the road. It was held by the justices and affirmed on appeal that these wheels did not comply with the Act and that the nine-inch width had to be in the form of a continuous tyre, apart from necessary joints, round the whole periphery of the wheel.

Section 32 gave county authorities the power to make byelaws requiring locomotives, other than those used for agriculture, to be licensed annually at a yearly rate not exceeding ten pounds. This obviously bore very hardly upon an owner in say London who might use his engine within a few miles radius in Essex, Kent, Surrey and Middlesex. To meet this kind of case, the Local Government Board wrote a circular letter to the Clerks of the Peace of Counties, under the date of September 18, 1878 saying:

"In determining the fee to be paid it must be borne in mind that there will be many instances in which the same locomotive will be used in more than one county, and special provision will have to be made for these cases. This may perhaps be done by requiring the full fee, whatever may be the amount fixed, to be paid in the county where the licence is taken out, the county officer obtaining from the other counties, the necessary licences afterwards and paying

over to them their proportion of the aggregate fee".

This arrangement did not work well and gave opportunities for endless procrastination and obstruction by county authorities. It was stated* that it sometimes took an owner three months to obtain from a Court of Quarter Sessions a licence to travel on the highway and that the owner of an engine situated on the borders of two or more counties was often required to pay the full £10 duty to each county.

On the principle that it was better to hang together than to hang separately owners of traction engines had begun to form trade associations. In Kent, the owners formed the Kent County Engine Owners Association of which for years thirteen firms were principal members, all of whose names were practically household words among the engine-men of Kent—J. Robson & Sons, Henry Chapman, Walter Arnold & Sons, Chittenden & Simmonds Ltd, Thomas Wood & Sons, S. Sladden, Church & Goodhew, W. Morris, Aveling & Porter Ltd, Jesse Ellis & Co Ltd, Wingham Agricultural Implement Co, Sidney Neame, and Barmby & Wyles Ltd. Though the idea of mutual protection was good the association was too small in scope, with an annual subscription income of only about £25, to form an effective fighting force and though it was pleasant for the proprietors to meet from time to time to lunch or dine together, to take perhaps a little wine or whisky and to swap comments and advice, something on a national scale was needed.

The "something" that emerged was the National Traction Engine Owners' and Users' Association founded on December 6, 1893, on the initiative of the Kent County Association which had convened the meeting from which

*Report of the Select Committee on Traction Engines on Roads, July 1, 1896.

it emerged and had booked Sadlers Wells Theatre for the occasion. Mr. A. G. Boscawen, the MP for Tonbridge, was persuaded to take the chair and the meeting was supported by a group of engine manufacturers—Ransomes, Sims, Hornsby, Aveling and Burrell. When the chairman put the proposition that a National Association be formed it was seconded by John Allen of Oxford. Mr Boscawen, J. E. Ransome, Thomas Aveling, John McLaren, R. H. Fowler and Robert Eddison (both of John Fowler & Co), Charles Burrell, and Edwin Foden were all members of the first committee with seven members of the Kent Association and two from elsewhere.

The Association was particularly fortunate in its choice of a legal adviser, William Joynson-Hicks, later knighted, who finally became Lord Brentford. "Jix's" first great service to traction engines was to marshall the evidence

presented to the Select Committee during the first half of 1896 and which was largely responsible for the favourable report delivered by the Committee.

The Locomotives on Highways Act of 1896 relieved the traction engine finally of the need for the lookoutman twenty yards ahead. It also recognised that the light vehicles then being produced, varying from motor cars up to light traction engines, could not with justice be lumped into the same class as the heavy haulage engine, by removing the necessity for manning by three men and by raising the speed limit— so far as light traction engines were concerned to six miles per hour.

In moving the second reading of the Bill in the House, Mr Chaplin expressed the belief that the light road locomotive might become a dangerous rival of the light railway; that it would develop a big industry, tend to decrease

Mann & Charlesworth was re-constituted as Mann's Patent Steam Cart & Wagon Company, concentrating upon the products named in the title. However tractors based upon the steam cart design were also made and No 611 is seen here hauling two self-binders at the RASE trails   [J. T. Newman

railway fares and prove to be of great advantage to agricultural interests. The House received this ludicrous suggestion with amusement! The mood of Parliament was, however, becoming steadily more favourable to steam upon the road.

The report of the 1896 Select Committee shows a real appreciation of the frustration experienced by the owners and drivers of road locomotives faced with the handiwork of the sixty to seventy local authorities which had chosen to make byelaws regulating the hours of travelling or use upon the highway of engines or their right to cross bridges. Among the many sensible recommendations made by the committee, whose work was embodied in the Locomotive Act 1898, was the raising of the speed limit in towns and villages to 3mph, the use of any form of wheel approved by the Local Government Board, the fixing of a duty of £10 per annum in the county of origin for weights up to ten tons with a payment of 2s 6d for each incursion into any other county it visited. The Act exempted steam rollers from duty and gave a definition to the class of "agricultural engines" which were, as they had always been, not liable to either licensing or tax. The oversight of local byelaws by the Local Government Board was also strengthened whilst the recovery of expenses for damage done by "extra-ordinary traffic" was made recoverable in the County Court or High Court instead of before the Justices of the Peace who on the whole had been found to be resolute enemies of the steam engine.

Extraordinary traffic was defined by Lord Justice Bowen (in Hill v. Thomas) as follows: "Extraordinary traffic is really a carriage of articles over the road at either one or more times, which is so exceptional in the quality or quantity of goods carried, or in the mode or time of user of the road, as substantially to increase the burden imposed by ordinary traffic on the road, and to cause damage and expense thereby beyond what is common". Some extraordinary decisions were given from time to time on cases of alleged extraordinary traffic and before a bench of magistrates who were all local ratepayers it was a difficult charge to answer conclusively.

It was on this matter of extraordinary traffic that Joynson-Hicks obtained a notable victory for engine owners in the case of Monmouth County Council v. Scott. Scott owned limestone quarries and had brought a traction engine into use to replace horses and carts for transport from quarry to station. The County Council sought and obtained an interim injunction restraining Scott from using the engine on the ground that it was *per se* a nuisance.

At the principal hearing before Mr Justice Jelf, Joynson-Hicks put a skilful case backed by carefully assembled witnesses. The judge found that the disrepair of the road was due in part to the engine, in part to the horse hauled stone traffic and in part by the ordinary traffic but chiefly to the County Council's failure to maintain the road in a fit state to bear the traffic that it ought to have expected to use it. This verdict was no use to the plaintiffs, who appealed, only to have the appeal dismissed and the injunction dissolved. Scott was furthermore awarded damages in compensation for the period during which he was unable to make use of the engine.

The Association was equally happy in its choice of a consulting engineer—the late Henry Howard Humphreys. His great strength was his durability under cross-examination. In one case he was being closely examined by a hostile counsel without marked effect. Had he not heard, questioned counsel, the evidence of Mr X and Mr Y as to the road being in a dangerous condition? "Yes", replied H.H.H., "but if a platoon of archangels were to come into this court and say the road was dangerous I would still believe my own senses".

The attitude of county officers towards engines is illustrated by a report given by the County Surveyor of Kent, Henry Maybury, in 1907.

One hundred and seven engines were licenced in Kent in the preceding year, 120 day permits were issued and agricultural engine licences totalled 137. This traffic, he commented, "is most damaging to the roads whilst the fees accruing therefrom are ridiculously small. Upon payment of half-a-crown an engine may traverse the whole county doing damage to the extent of hundreds of pounds." He made the point that the total revenue from day permits was £15 from which he deduced the conclusion that "for the benefit of a comparatively few people, the whole of the ratepayers of the county have to find large sums of money year after year to make good the damage caused". Maybury underwent a subsequent change of heart and later became Chairman of the Main Roads Board.

To be fair to the surveyors, however, it must be admitted that engines could, and sometimes did, do damage to roads, occasionally even deliberate damage, as in 1910 when John Penfold, the Kent showman was summoned at Sittingbourne for damaging the roadway at King's Ferry, Iwade. As his vans were too high to pass under the railway bridge he dug trenches thirty feet long and a foot deep in the road surface. He did this once on his way out on August 2 and again on his return on the 19th. Surprisingly the episode cost him only £3 4s 0d including his fine, costs and damages.

The Kent County Council may have been able to experience a little fellow feeling for the engine owner exposed to the prejudices of magistrates. In 1906 a cottage at Shatterling was burned out because one of their drivers put hot clinkers on the road side waste near to it. This cost the council £150. In December, 1907 it was prosecuted at Tonbridge for allowing, by the default of its driver, George Bailey, one of its locomotives to emit smoke in Tonbridge on November 7. The summons had been twice adjourned but this time the case was heard and a conviction recorded. The newspaper report of the evidence said that:

"According to Sergeant Eaglen and P.C. Martin on November 7th they saw the engine coming from the Medway Wharf almost obscured by its own smoke. The sergeant shouted and the constable blew his whistle but the driver, instead of stopping, proceeded at a speed which made it impossible for them to overtake it. The sergeant had, however, seen the number. Next morning the driver, on being spoken to, said he did not understand the signal or he would have stopped.

MR BRACHER, FOR THE K.C.C. (to the sergeant): Do you mean to say that you could not overtake him?

WITNESS: No sir, the engine can go five miles an hour and I can only go two. (Laughter).

MR BRACHER: That is very funny.

WITNESS: No, it is not funny. A sergeant could not go up High Street in uniform at five miles an hour without bringing everyone out into the street.

AFTER P.C. MARTIN'S EVIDENCE MR BRACHER ASKED: If Sergeant Eaglen is not a sprinter, why didn't you go after the defendant?

WITNESS: I remained on duty in the street and the sergeant went after him.

MR BRACHER: At two miles an hour?

WITNESS: Something about that sir. (Laughter)."

Despite the farce a conviction was registered.

Magistrates were in fact often so hopelessly biased that no engine driver or owner could expect a fair hearing. Captain Mansell of the Hythe County Bench, in 1907 observed during the hearing of a case of obstruction, "Traction engines are a great nuisance at the best of times and if the engine drivers do not take care they are unbearable". Captain Baldwin concurred, adding, "Traction engines are horrible things".

In any search through local papers a few types of charge crops up again and again against engine drivers—emitting dark smoke, obstruction, blowing off steam on the road, and using prohibited roads or bridges. Against owners quite the most damaging thing was the claim for "extraordinary traffic". The costs

F

charged against engine traffic were relatively enormous. When Mr W. Astor carried out the reconstruction of Hever Castle in 1908 he contributed the sum of £2,000 toward reinstatement of the damage to the roads caused by the engines hauling the materials. At this time the Surveyor of a rural district council was paid £250 a year so the magnitude of the sum can be gauged. Few settlements of this size were reached but sums of £50 to £100 were common. In June, 1904 William Lambert of Horsmonden had to pay the Cranbrook Rural District Council £55 1s 9d for damage caused to Water Lane, Hawkhurst, by carting 235 tons of manure over it—an increase of four shillings and eightpence per ton in the price. Perhaps the most surprising cases occurred where a district council brought an action against a county council for damage caused when carting road stone for country roads—a Gilbertian situation where the only profit was to the lawyers and the public, whether from one pocket or another footed the entire bill.

World War I seems finally to have convinced minor authorities that heavy haulage on the road had come to stay. Claims for extraordinary traffic declined during the 'twenties and had all but disappeared by the 'thirties.

the loads, including the proprietor's caravan, overturning. Thomas Bone, a twenty-four-years-old comedian attached to the show, died from a fractured skull, Mrs Hobson, another woman and two young men travelling in the van were injured but the driver and steersman seem to have escaped.

Accidents were rarer on ascending hills but even here there could be trouble. If the loads proved too much to take up together, which was a not uncommon occurrence when the roads were greasy, they had to be divided. Provided the train was divided on level ground or adequately scotched up the manoeuvre could usually be accomplished safely. If the scotching went wrong trouble followed as it did early one Friday morning in 1908 in North Street, Strood, Kent. An Aveling & Porter road engine belonging to Chittenden & Simmonds (now part of the Amalgamated Roadstone Corporation) of Wrotham, with three eight-ton loads of stone behind it was brought to a stand by the greasy wood block surface. The driver decided to divide the train and take up each wagon separately. This he did successfully with the first two, but as he was backing up to the third the scotch became dislodged, possibly because he set up a little sharply and at once

Not all the troubles of engines arose from the law, however. Runaways accounted for a high proportion of the accidents that happened to engines if not of those who manned them. An engine could get out of control by tackling the descent of a steep hill in high gear with a heavy load but usually the worst that happened was that it could not be stopped. Sometimes nevertheless matters got really out of hand as when Ernest Hobson's "electrical hippodrome" loads and the engine hauling them ran away downhill at Radley, Leeds. The driver stuck to the engine and steered it away from a horse and cart but hit a telegraph pole, bringing down the pole and the wires after which it collided with a wall in which the engine embedded itself,

The consequence of the running away of a Fowler single-cylinder plougher owned by Thomas Wood & Son. The date is said to be in the 'eighties and the situation reputed to be Dartford

[Thomas Wood & Son

the laden wagon was away downhill towards the High Street. The three men could do nothing but watch, expecting it to burst disastrously upon the traffic in the High Street and fearful of the havoc it would cause. Outside the Three Gardeners, however, some bump in the road deflected the forecarriage causing the wagon to slew across the road and smash into the front of No 19 North Street, where the elderly householder, Miss Alice Cork was asleep, to be awakened by the cataclysmic sounds of sundering timbers, falling slates and collapsing brickwork.

Another accident, not far distant in either time or place, happened to one of the Butler engines from Chart Sutton near Maidstone, when descending Boxley Hill with three loads of stone, all with the wheels locked in skid pans. Despite this the engine could not hold them and the loads jacknifed on to it. Frank Butler, who was driving stuck to it but Harry Baker, his mate, tried to jump off and was fatally injured by being caught between the engine and the leading truck.

The driver and mate were more fortunate in an accident involving another Chittenden & Simmonds engine at Vigo Hill near West Malling, Kent, in May 1907. In this case the trucks were empty, despite which the train got out of control and the engine turned over, fortunately giving the crew no worse injuries than a broken ankle and a dislocated shoulder. Even more alarming was the runaway of an engine belonging to John Mansfield at Cullompton, Devon, the year before. Though it happened on a hill the cause of accident was the steering wheel coming off. The engine ran into the hedge and turned right over demolishing the canopy and scattering pieces of the engine for a dozen yards. Again by good fortune the crew escaped with their lives though at the expense of scalds and injuries.

The stone sett roads of industrial Lancashire and Yorkshire were particularly treacherous to steel-wheeled traction engines, the smooth, hard setts providing a surface on which the wheels struck and slid. Arthur Fay tells the story* of James Crighton's bioscope show narrowly being saved from disaster in a sett paved road in the Colne Valley district. In response to the engine driver's call for brakes— two pips on the whistle—the brakeman on each load wound on the brakes. At once the whole train began to slide over the setts and

*"Some Bioscope Shows and their Engines".

Richardson & Co's (of Epsom) Burrell road engine No 2243 after a runaway in February, 1911 down Epsom Road, Guildford when travelling with furniture from Epsom to Southampton

The other side of the same accident

though the driver eased off the engine brakes in an endeavour to regain control the train continued to gain on him. The episode ended with the locomotive in the gutter, the organ truck alongside it and the rest of the train snaked across the road, a situation that gave a fair indication of impending disaster almost miraculously retrieved, though four or five hours of hard work were required to reassemble the train at the foot of the hill.

Another failure which gave rise to runaways was loss of a driving pin. This happened to a single crank compound Burrell owned by Stan Smith of Cressing on a hill at Bocking, Essex, during 1943. The engine, which was hauling a threshing drum and elevator on which a number of men, including several German prisoners of war were riding, was being driven by its owner when he noticed that the speed of the road wheels was gaining on that of the engine. Looking down he saw the pin pro-

The result of a runaway at Church Enstone, Oxon. Both the distressed Fowler road locomotive and the Fowler single-cylinder plougher sent to the rescue were owned by the Oxfordshire Steam Ploughing Co

The late Dan Crittal and the men who righted Stan Smith's Burrell after its upset at Bocking, Essex, during the late War

truding and, leaving the engine to the steersman he jumped down on to the road and ran alongside trying to push the pin back without success. The engine gained speed, struck the bank and as with Mansfield's engine turned over upsetting the drum and scattering the passengers over the road. By great good fortune no one was hurt and the late Dan Crittall retrieved the engine using a big crawler tractor.

An accident happened in 1914 to one of the Tasker tractors owned by G. E. Farrant of Tunbridge Wells. The tractor was returning

The result of an accident in 1916 to a Tasker compound tractor owned by G. E. Farrant of Tunbridge Wells. It was on the return journey empty from Folkestone and was ascending Quarry Hill, Tonbridge, when the offside (fixed) wheel came off with the consequence shown. Mr Farrant, the driver, escaped but the mate was trapped and killed. The wheel was secured by a stud in the end of the axle with a washer and nut, which was prevented from turning by a hexagon locking place and a stud. This broke, the plate moved, the nut came undone and the wheel came off

[F. Lambert collection

from Folkestone with an empty furniture van belonging to Harris of Tunbridge Wells. At the foot of Quarry Hill, Tonbridge, no more than five miles from home, the tractor lost a rear wheel, turned over and crushed the steersman to death. Sid Lambert, Farrant's present works foreman, went to the scene with his late father to right the engine. The accident was caused by the method used to secure the wheel, namely a stud in the end of the axle with a plate and nut, the nut being secured by a locking plate fixed in its turn by a stud and cotter. The stud sheared, the locking plate fell off, the nut unwound and the wheel was lost. Taskers subsequently altered this fixing to the collar and cotter method.

Collapse of the road or of bridges was another fruitful source of mishaps. The agricultural engine pottering around a district that the driver knew like the back of his hand rarely ran into this sort of trouble, except for the rare case when a bridge thought to be substantial collapsed. When engines moved further afield the situation was not the same. The national firms of the calibre of Pickfords or Norman Box when moving the very largest loads used to survey the route to be followed checking clearances and load capacities. Most troubles happened with the ordinary load which took the driver off the roads he knew. An accident of this type befell an Aveling engine belonging to Chittenden & Simmonds, of Maidstone, in the early 1900s. Returning to Maidstone from the direction of West Farleigh, south of the Medway, he lost his way and was directed by a passer-by down the road that led to the weak wooden bridge at Barming. Trapped with his big Aveling road engine and two trucks in the narrow bridge approach he had the choice of attempting the bridge or sending for help to pull back the trucks and allow him to turn. By ill-fortune he took the first choice with the result that both he and the engine and trucks crashed through the bridge into the river.

Not less catastrophic in their effects than runaways were boiler explosions, though they were certainly less numerous. One of the best known boiler explosions happened on December 3, 1880 to an Aveling & Porter traction engine built in 1877 and owned by Jesse Ellis & Co of Maidstone. The engine was working at night—the explosion happened at 3 am—carting what was described as "manure" but is believed to have been night soil. The driver, a young man named Moses Martin, had stopped in Mill Street, Maidstone, to enable a lamp to be relit and was restarting when the boiler exploded with such violence that the engine was completely destroyed. Martin and Harry Reader, the flagman, survived but Frank Underwood the mate was killed—Martin being subsequently tried for his manslaughter. Both Martin and Reader were injured by flying fragments and the buildings flanking the street —a builder's yard and St Anne's Church— were scored by the pieces as well as having the windows broken. Jesse Ellis' daughter Mabel remembers looking at the marks as a small child and thinking "one of our engines did that". Her father had left the previous day for Oxford where he was to attend an auction on December 3. Mrs Ellis telegraphed the auctioneer and the first announcement from the rostrum at the auction asked if Mr Jesse Ellis was present as if so would he please return to Maidstone where one of his engines had exploded during the night.

The explosion had been caused by excessive pressure in a boiler which had already been weakened by having a crack in the firebox repaired with copper studs, tapped in overlapping and peened tight. The ferrules on the spring balance safety valves had been tampered with after it left the maker's works—with the owner's tacit if not explicit consent—to an extent where it was possible to dead lock the valves.

There is little doubt that Jesse Ellis and his workmen were doing only what dozens if not hundreds of others were doing and continued to do as long as steam lasted, namely to take unpardonable liberties with its latent power

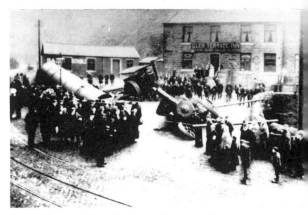

An accident at Waterfoot near Rawtenstall, Lancs, that shows the peril of weak bridges to traction engines

both by the manner of making repairs and by subjecting boilers to pressures for which they were not designed. In the case of the men, ignorance and occasionally sloth, were to blame. Without informed consideration of the possible consequences some drivers would increase the boiler pressure when they found themselves in an awkward spot—the roads might be soft or the gradient too severe—and the amount of work to be got through in a day was large. Owners too often had remarkably scant knowledge of the effects of excessive pressure and wastage on a boiler. The story is told of the owner being examined at the enquiry into the explosion of one of his engines. Was he not aware, he was asked, that the ruptured plate was as thin as it was and that it needed patching. Yes, he replied, he had known about it and had caused a patch to be made ready for instant use, should it ever become necessary!

Jesse Ellis probably could not claim to have been ignorant of the consequences of overloading safety valves and in the case we are considering, matters had probably gone rather further than he intended. After the ferrules had been shortened to allow the pressure to be raised, it had been found that the balances were a little light and accordingly a washer had been inserted under the springs limiting the travel to only $\frac{5}{16}$ in beyond the 120lb mark. Though he was, like many Victorian employers, stern and domineering, outwardly at least, with the men he employed, he did not take them on and stand them off at will and, in consequence many of his men stayed with him for long periods—some even for the whole of the thirty-odd years or so that he was in business. He might well have condoned the use from time to time of a pressure 25lb in excess of the proper working pressure of 100lb sq in, when an engine was in a hole, on a soft road, on a gradient where a lesser pressure

The consequence of the explosion of the boiler of a Fowler ploughing engine owned by Pamplin Bros of Cherryhinton, Cambs., in 1904. The explosion was the result of a very hard pull on the cultivator proving too much for a boiler severely weakened by corrosion

would have meant dividing the load or in a town where to allow the valves to blow meant risking prosecution but he was certainly most unlikely to have agreed to a situation where the valves could be locked. Owners were subjected besides to heavy stresses by the commercial conditions of the time—competition was extreme and in market towns like Maidstone the onset of the agricultural depression was making money scarce, all of which was calculated to make them turn a blind eye to over economical repairs or to practices which enabled just a little more to be got through in a working day.

Another pernicious practice that caused trouble was replacing the fusible plug by an iron plug. From time to time a driver would run out the fusible plug—sometimes innocently by a false gauge glass reading or an unexpected steep descent but often by neglect, not infrequently failure to detect a shortage of liquor within the boiler being the consequence of over much inside the driver. If a spare was not carried or had been run out already to pop in a bolt or an iron plug saved a tedious march to the nearest blacksmith and awkward explanations to the owner. To use an iron plug for a few miles in an emergency was thus possibly excusable—to do it for weeks was folly so incredible that it is difficult to understand how it could have gone on; but it did.

Yet another trouble caused by water was priming, the carrying over of boiler water into the cylinder. Getting the engine head down with a full boiler led easily to this trouble if the throttle was open and a clumsy or tipsy driver shunting about on a sloping site was almost bound to contrive this sooner or later. Priming with clean water in sufficient quantities could lead, in an engine with well fitting piston rings and tight cylinder taps, to a cylinder cover being burst off by the pressure of the incompressible water trapped behind the advancing piston. If this did not happen the draining off of the water through the taps and the running of additional cylinder oil into the cylinder from

the lubricator was sufficient to correct the trouble. Far more pernicious, however, was the priming caused not so much by mishandling as by the filling of the boiler with contaminated water. Since outside the towns engines were nearly always watered from ponds and streams and only rarely from wells or rainwater butts they inevitably drew up a certain amount of

The famous accident to the Hackbridge transformer at Cobham in 1938, the last major pitch-in that happened to steam heavy haulage. The accident was said to have been the result of a steering chain failing on the leading engine. Two transformers had been moved safely—the accident happened with the third. E. W. Rudd was the contractor but had called in help from Coulson of Park Royal and J. Hickey & Sons of Cheshunt. The engines involved were Coulson's Fowler No JF 9904 (leading), Rudd's Fowler No JF 14921 (second) and, at the rear, Hickey's Burrell City of London

gritty sediment with the water, some of which found its way into the boiler. A fill from a source contaminated by ducks, by domestic waste water or dairy washings or by any kind of oil or grease would set off a kind of foaming action on the boiler contents which tended to carry in it gritty scum that once in the cylinder would cause trouble by scoring and abrasion. The best the driver could do on the road was to keep the water level as low as possible and endeavour to blow out the filth through the taps, partially flushing the cylinder with several heavy dosages of cylinder oil. Long term it would

have paid to empty down the boiler, draw the piston and thoroughly clean both it and the cylinder. Regrettably this rarely happened and wear resulted.

Though it rarely led to accidents and seldom to damage beyond burned firebars coal trouble probably caused as many day-to-day bothers for enginemen as the remaining causes lumped together. Coal does not stand up well to frost or long storage in the open and as a firm worked down to the bottom of its coal stack steaming troubles could follow the increase in the slack content from firstly the poorer combustion of

The consequences of pulling too close to the edge of a country road. An un-named Fowler in trouble near Talyllyn sixty years ago

The pleasures of the travelling life. N. Tomlinson's McLaren haulage tractor set fast in Locke Park, Barnsley during "Joy Week" in 1936

[Cyclist

the slack and secondly the amount of clinker it produced. Slack from the non-coking coals would merely fall unburnt through the bars, denuding the fire-bed and filling the ashpan with a secondary fire. This in turn led to over-heating and consequent burning of the bars.

As the coal for threshing engines had to be found, as a rule, by the customer the fuel they were presented with varied in the extreme. Within a circuit of a few miles a driver might encounter hard Welsh, a South Yorkshire steam coal, a Derbyshire house coal or the refuse of the domestic coal shed. In the early 'thirties when farmers were really put to scraping the bottom of the barrel contractors were faced with some remarkable extremes. Since all the fuels listed above require a different spacing of the firebars and a different firing technique it is not to be wondered at that very varied results were produced.

Generally speaking to fire a hard coal with a lower proportion of volatiles a good thick fire must be kept up with carefully and regularly spaced bars not more than $\frac{3}{8}$in apart at any point, kept clean and with a clear ashpan. A fire of this type suited a Great Western Railway King Class locomotive very well on a journey calling for consistent effort over long spells. It therefore answered equally well for threshing where the engines worked con-sistently. Where it brought problems was on the road. Being slower to ignite and needing a hot fire to ignite it, it did not allow the driver to vary his fire to anything like the extent to which he could do so with a softer coal. Consequently, though well provided with steam when it was needed, the driver found himself with an embarrassing superfluity of it when he did not want it. At such times, he might be moving slowly through town traffic or running with shut throttle downhill. In the heyday of the traction engine when the police were ready to detect and the benches were quick to convict any driver guilty of blowing off steam in a town this characteristic of the hard coal became so onerous as to disqualify it in the eyes of many owners, especially those intimately involved in the working of their engines. The author's friend Charles Hooker kept his hard coal for the kitchen range and used best house coal on his engines. As it caught easily he had good control over the size of his fire and by firing a little at a time and regulating the top air he managed to prevent dark smoke, the other fruitful cause of prosecutions.

In fact to burn hard Welsh coal successfully on a road engine required an ashpan with minimal air leaks, so that combustion could be rigidly controlled by a well fitted damper, and close fitting doors on the firebox and smoke-box. Regrettably these conditions were very rarely found on engines in commercial use.

Fowler road engine No 14734 (John Read, Haywood Lodge, Hereford) overturned just outside Hereford just before World War II

EPILOGUE

Why the Traction Engine has gone out of use

WHEN it is healthy, design never stands still, however slowly it may appear to travel. The English traction engine, as we have seen, evolved in circumstances where the incentives for new design were minimal. Best steam coal was ten shillings a ton at the pit head, skilled engineers' labour was cheap and very plentiful and neither circumstance, at the beginning of this century, appeared likely to change.

In consequence, the traction engine designer had no need to consider alternative fuels nor the need for assembly line methods. The latter, however, were vitally necessary to American manufacturing industry, where the skilled mechanic was far more of a rarity, and were brought to an advanced level before 1914 by Henry Ford.

Before that date, paraffin-engined tractors had been put to work by English manufacturers including Marshall, Sons & Co Ltd, of Gainsborough, already well established makers of steam traction engines. All, however, were made on the traditional principles of assembly in the same way as the traction engines and were built to the same standards of durability, being in consequence both expensive and heavy. Nevertheless, they had, in theory at least, the advantage of instant availability.

The application of Ford's principles to tractor making produced the Fordson tractor. The same ideas in the hands of the International Harvester Company produced a comparable machine. Each of these was capable of doing virtually any of the work done by the farm horse—carting, ploughing, harrowing, drilling or haymaking—and, in addition, could drive a saw-bench, chaff cutter or hammer-mill. Moreover, it was found that it could also power a threshing machine—not very well at first because it did not govern accurately but it was seen to have definite possibilities.

Tractors did not require a man to rise an hour and a half before his fellows to raise steam and could be stopped and started at will, at least in the brochures. Readers who have been involved in starting a recalcitrant Fordson on a cold, damp morning, ending with the magneto being detached and baked in the oven, will have a laugh at this statement but the essence of truth is there.

When Denzil Lobley of Richard Garrett & Sons Ltd encountered his first Fordson in 1918, he wrote to his Engineering Director (W. J. Marshall), as he said, "For the edification of the agricultural community in the works", giving technical particulars of the new tractor. He concluded, "These figures give me furiously to think as to the future, if any, of steam . . .".

Though the motor vehicle was by that time well entrenched in road haulage, it had not made any appreciable impression on agriculture or heavy haulage and great goodwill still prevailed towards the steam engine. Had traction engine builders been able, therefore, to produce an answer to the advantages of the motor tractor, light-weight, low cost and ready availability, they would probably have met with a warm response.

In the event, they did not produce such an answer. Why they did not is a complex question. Some firms building traction engines in 1914 were doing so on a very limited scale, such firms as Fowell, Sparrow and Wantage Engineering building only two or three engines a year as they were ordered. Other firms, such as, for instance, Tasker of Andover, were producing on a larger scale but with obsolete methods. Yet again, several of the progressive firms, notably Garrett of Leiston and Clayton & Shuttleworth of Leiston, who had made big strides in standardisation and who might have gone on to really modern methods, had been trading extensively with Russia and had lost vast sums when the Soviet Government repudiated foreign debts after the Revolution. Marshall of Gainsborough was a firm tolerably open to new ideas and was receptive to the internal combustion engine and thus, from the steam point of view, prepared to sell the pass.

To combine into larger manufacturing units

Aveling & Porter crane engine No 2651 near the end of its life when owned by C. Taylor, an engine dealer and scrap merchant at Redbourn, Herts. The cleading sheets are rusted through and the wooden lagging is showing below the cylinder block

[J. P. Mullett]

Allchin G.P. engine No 1539 in August 1953, with 2146 in the background   [J. F. Clay

was an essential and the formation of Agricultural & General Engineers, combining the firms of Charles Burrell & Sons Ltd, Richard Garrett & Sons Ltd, Aveling & Porter Ltd and Davey Paxman & Co Ltd with several makers in other or allied fields, was a step in the right direction. The methods of management used and the directors appointed were such, however, that it perished from its internal stresses.

It thus fell to the Sentinel Waggon Works to be the sole company engaged upon the production of progressive designs of steam vehicles. Most other makers continued to offer their 1914 designs with minimal changes and steadily decreasing orders until about 1932 when the diesel engine and the Slump burst upon the scene. Very heavy haulage until then

had been a field in which steam could hold its own against the petrol engine but the diesel could compete and the last barrier was breached.

The advent of the Salter Report and the consequent increased road tax on steam vehicles in 1932 added to the distresses of the traction engine, though not altogether unjustly. The fuel of motor vehicles was taxed whereas coal was not. Consequently, steam vehicles, until 1932, were paying far less tax than motors, which might have been justifiable on the grounds that the use of coal supported a native, and ailing, industry but not otherwise.

As a result of the three agencies of financial stringency, intensive competition and stagnation of design, the old established firms of engine builders succumbed one by one, some to

total extinction, others to reconstruction under
new managements whose programmes excluded
steam.

Steam wagons and road locomotives fell in
the largest numbers during the 1930s. By the
end of the 'thirties, the rot was beginning to
hit the showground and the threshing trade
and had bitten deep into steam ploughing, but
the onset of World War II and the postwar
shortages kept most of the surviving engines
at work for another seven or eight years.
Thereafter, heavy tractors were thrown on the
market by war stores disposal which led to the
end of steam on fairgrounds whilst the advent
of the combine harvester gradually obliterated
threshing by steam or any other power. Steam
rolling, which had stood up well to the advance
of motor power, gradually gave way as drivers
oecame harder and dearer to find, few young
men of the 1950s being willing to accept the
harsh disciplines of steam driving.

At the time of writing a limited number of
steam rollers is still in regular work together
with a small band of steam ploughing engines,
the latter surviving because there are certain
roles they can do economically and well.
In June, 1969, the author's company employed
a steam ploughing engine to haul a heavy roller
up and down a precipitous slope in Lancashire.
Several sets are employed by other firms on the
dredging of lakes and ponds and there is still
steam ploughing done. How long steam con-
tinues at work depends on how long it is
possible to keep existing engines in working
trim now that no new ones can be made.